BOLLINGEN SERIES LXV

ARCHETYPAL IMAGES IN GREEK RELIGION

Volume 3

C. Kerényi

ASKLEPIOS

Archetypal Image of the Physician's Existence

TRANSLATED FROM THE GERMAN

BY *Ralph Manheim*

BOLLINGEN SERIES LXV · 3

PANTHEON BOOKS

THIS IS VOLUME THREE IN A GROUP OF STUDIES OF
ARCHETYPAL IMAGES IN GREEK RELIGION
WHICH CONSTITUTE THE SIXTY-FIFTH PUBLICATION
IN A SERIES SPONSORED BY AND PUBLISHED FOR
BOLLINGEN FOUNDATION

Originally published in German as Der göttliche Arzt:
Studien über Asklepios und seine Kultstätten, by Ciba Ltd.,
Basel, 1947 (also in French: Le Médecin divin); revised
edition, © 1956, by Wissenschaftliche Buchgesellschaft,
Darmstadt, and Hermann Gentner Verlag, Darmstadt

Library of Congress Catalogue Card Number: 59–13516
MANUFACTURED IN THE UNITED STATES OF AMERICA
BY KINGSPORT PRESS, INC., KINGSPORT, TENNESSEE
DESIGNED BY ANDOR BRAUN

CONTENTS

LIST OF ILLUSTRATIONS

After 1500 B.C.   Demonstrable existence of Greek mythology, to whose flowering in Thessaly belongs the centaur Chiron, Asklepios' instructor in medicine. Cf. "The Origins in Thessaly," p. 87

Before 600 B.C.   Era of Homer and Hesiod, the most ancient sources for Asklepios and his family. Cf. "Hero Physicians and the Physician of the Gods in Homer," p. 70

600–400 B.C.   Era of the Asklepiads at Kos; ca. 460–377, lifetime of Hippokrates; shortly afterwards, foundation of an Asklepieion on Kos, in the sacred grove of Apollo Kyparissios. Cf. "The Sons of Asklepios on Kos," p. 47

500–300 B.C.   First period of the Asklepieion at Epidauros; 420, foundation of a temple of Asklepios at Athens; ca. 300, inscriptions commemorating the "Cures of Apollo and Asklepios," and the paean of Isyllos at Epidauros, chief source for this epoch. Cf. "Epidauros," p. 18

291 B.C.   Foundation of the Asklepieion on the Tiber Island in Rome; decisive step toward the dissemination of the cult of Asklepios in the Roman empire. Cf. "Asklepios in Rome," p. 3

IN THIS book I invite the reader to accompany me on a tour of the sites where the cult of Asklepios, god of medicine and god of the Greek physicians, was practiced. This is one way of approaching mythology and hence Asklepios; I do not claim that it is the only possible way, but I do believe that this approach will be of interest not only to those physicians and lovers of antiquity who happen to be interested in psychology but to many others as well. Other works on the same subject written at the same time have followed a different method, about which I should like to say a few words lest the reader be confused when he comes up against contradictory findings in an important point.

The works to which I am referring are excellent collections of source material: the one, *Asclepius: A Collection and Interpretation of the Testimonies*, by Emma J. Edelstein and Ludwig Edelstein, is a compendium of the literary sources and inscriptions; the other, *Kunst and Heiltum* ("Art and Medicine"), by Ulrich Hausmann, is devoted to an important group of religious monuments. Both works were written on the basis of a conviction that is frequently encountered in such studies. I have in mind the belief that since the turn of the century the main problems regarding Asklepios and his tradition have been definitely cleared up. According to this theory, even the beginnings are explained by the fact that in the Iliad the future god of physicians is mentioned only as the father of two heroes who practice the healer's art, Machaon and Podaleirios; that he is represented as an "excellent physician" but otherwise merely as a warrior king like many others. Because the Homeric poems say nothing about his divinity or his myth, it was inferred that Asklepios had been a "physician hero" in his native place, the Thessalian city of Trikka, also mentioned in the Iliad. According to this theory, he was elevated to divine rank only later or—in case he had after all been a god in some remote past—re-elevated. In any event, he must for centuries have been worshiped only as a hero, as a mortal to whom a hero cult had been attached. And this worship, this cult practiced over a hero's grave, where perhaps healing dreams were already dreamed and cures were effected, is represented as the beginning. Studies of this type on Asklepios take this purely hypothetical beginning as their starting point.

✶

It should be stressed that works such as these two do not derive their value from this hypothesis regarding the beginning and source of the myth and could perfectly well dispense with it. The weakness of the hypothesis, which was accepted as dogma even earlier, is easily shown. To be perfectly accurate, we cannot even glean the information that Asklepios was a "physician hero" at Trikka from the Iliad. The Homeric epic says nothing about *any* cult but merely calls him an excellent physician; consequently it is impossible to say what cult it passes over in silence, whether only a hero cult or perhaps after all the cult of a god. A hero cult can indeed be interpreted as an enhanced cult of the dead, but the cult of a so-called chthonian god can also be regarded as an enhanced hero cult. How can one draw distinctions on the strength of what is not said and assert that what Homer passes over in silence is a hero cult? How can one infer that the cult of a chthonian god Asklepios was not yet in existence because the Iliad does not speak of it?

Homer's silence can only be understood as a reflection of the form which the Homeric poems were consciously bringing to Greek religion. The authors cited do not interpret it in this light and have the greatest difficulty in explaining how Asklepios' fame as a great god made its appearance in literature so late. True, they no longer maintain—as Wilamowitz still did—that his divinity was invented by priests at Epidauros.[2] But it is hardly better to attempt to solve the problem by referring to an Asklepios cult among the physicians, who in this version seem merely to replace the priests as the inventors of their hero's divinity.[3] It is utterly fanciful to derive a cult so rich in archaic elements as that of Asklepios from anything so vague as the cult of a physician hero at Trikka, whereas an interpretation of the post-Homeric sources and monuments, even if it involves mistakes, deals with a concrete tradition; moreover it gives to an essential part of the tradition, namely the mythological tradition, the attention which is its historical right.

∗

What a god meant to the Greeks is expressed by his myth or, stated in more elaborate words and images, by his mythology. If we wish to know who Asklepios was we must visit the sites of his cult and look into his mythology. There are two main reasons why the students of Asklepios, whose hypothesis of the origins of his cult has just been discussed, did not do this. The first reason springs from chronological misgivings. A little reflection shows these misgivings to be unfounded, for they are rooted in the tacit principle (generally followed by those students of religion who call their method historical) that what is not attested does not exist and comes into existence only with the first mention—although it is almost always a matter of accident when this first mention occurs. One is almost ashamed to take up arms against such a fallacy. Let it suffice to cite a master among historians of religion, Hermann Usener, who in an article on mythology [4] issues a warning against the false assumption that we have at our disposal virtually complete records of all epochs. It is perfectly childish, he declares, to assume that what we do not know cannot have been.

Actually we have only a post-Homeric tradition of the story of Asklepios' birth—and the birth is always the mythologem that most clearly reveals the character of a god. But the question is worth asking: was Homer the poet likely to honor this miraculous event with so much as an allusion? Everything about it is un-Homeric, but that does not prove it to be post-Homeric. The deciphering of the Mycenaean writing has added centuries to the span of pre-Homeric Greek religious history as a history showing names and dates; indeed, if we retain the customary dating of the Homeric poems (ninth to seventh century), it carries this history more than five hundred years farther back into the past. As was announced in the very first report, it has suddenly become possible to speak of Greek myths which "were already current from the fifteenth to the thirteenth century B.C." [5] The seeming impossibility of such a state of affairs had formerly led scholars to devise all sorts of imaginary lines of development, as in the case of Asklepios. And the same applies to Paieon, the physician of the gods in Homer, of whom we shall speak in Chapter IV. I should like to illustrate the present orientation of scholarship on the basis of this example before examining the myth of Asklepios from the new vantage point.

*

In the case of Paieon, an imaginary line of development was drawn from the cry "Paieon" in an equally imaginary magic incantation (imaginary because no word has come down to us of a magic incantation with this refrain) to the Homeric god Paieon. "Paieon has no cult," wrote Nilsson, who shared this view with certain of his predecessors; "he is nothing more than a personification of the healing incantation. This personification has become a physician." [6] Yet Paiavon was among the first names of Greek gods to be read in the Mycenaean inscriptions, and this is the form that "Paieon" would regularly take in the Mycenaean dialect. He had his place in the myths of the fifteenth to the thirteenth century and possessed his cult in Knossos, where he is mentioned as early as the fifteenth century. Roughly a thousand years later, a ritual song was still sung with the refrain: "May Paean never leave us, never cease!" We can only marvel at the persistence of this ancient cult. The god to whom it was devoted is drawn into the hymn far more than usual for a Greek god at that time. But this does not prove that he is, or ever was, the hymn itself. God and hymn are intimately linked in the cult. It is characteristic of Homeric theology, however, to regard the god as hovering high above the world of men and curing the gods on Olympos. My interpretation of him in Chapter IV (pp. 81 f.) is compatible with the new data.

Homer stood somewhat aloof even from paean singing—for him it was too ardent, too closely bound up with the god, the sun god Apollo, although the paean does occur as a song of thanksgiving and triumph in the Iliad. According to the Homeric hymn to Apollo (line 518), the Cretans were particularly adept singers of paeans: they had brought this song to Delphi in the train of Apollo—from the island where the name of Paiavon is attested. Homer was still more aloof toward Dionysos and his cult. And not because he was a relative late-comer in Greece, not because for Homer he was a new god. (This is another hypothesis that has collapsed today.) His name is attested in Mycenaean writing for the thirteenth century in Pylos in the southern Peloponnese, and assuredly his cult was limited neither in space nor in time to the cult in "Nestor's Palace" attested in this document. He too was among the myths of the fifteenth to the thirteenth century, but not one of the myths that Homer was likely to mention. It is only later that we encounter the fully developed myth—the mythologem of the god's birth and the tale of Dionysos and Ariadne—but in the Homeric poems we find allusions at least to the story of Ariadne. All these stories are variations on the same theme. Their core is assuredly pre-Homeric and at the same time they offer close parallels to the tale of Asklepios' birth. Only the names are different: in every case we have the same pre-Homeric, probably pre-Hellenic mythologem.

✱

Up to a certain point, Walter F. Otto in his *Dionysos* (p. 55) drew the parallel between the story of Ariadne and the mythologem of Asklepios' birth (by way of explaining the Homeric version of Ariadne's death). Carried to their conclusion, the parallels show the exact outlines of one of the most important mythologems in the whole history of Greek religion, the myth that was also proclaimed in the Eleusinian Mysteries. Homer did not recount this myth, although it was known to him. In the Odyssey (XI 320) it is related that Theseus could not have carried Ariadne far, for Artemis, at the behest of Dionysos, killed her on the isle of Dia. Here Otto recognized a parallel to the story of Koronis, mother of Asklepios. She was shot by Artemis at the instigation of Apollo, for she had been unfaithful to him, the father of her child. Thus there is a parallel even in the explanations of this incredible episode, all the essentials of which are perfectly parallel, or one might even say identical. On Koronis's pyre Asklepios was born: Apollo delivered the child from the dead mother. The mythologem of Ariadne's cult in Cyprus relates that she died in childbirth. And this cult had a sacred rite in which a young man imitated her birth pangs, taking them from her as it were and thus playing the role of Zeus. For in the birth of Dionysos Zeus did something similar: he took over Semele's pregnancy and completed it after she had given birth prematurely to Dionysos—not on a funeral pyre to be sure but even so amid flames, kindled by lightning.

Birth in death: that is what is proclaimed in this mythologem; and it is a truly un-Homeric myth. Only the name of the god thus born differs, in each case situating the impossible in contexts where it appears possible—just as the cure from fatal illness, for example, represents this possibility in the realm of Asklepios. In the cult of Ariadne on Cyprus the birth of Dionysos was re-enacted, though the child is not named. Dionysos comes into the world amid death not only in the Theban myth but also in the Orphic variant which has come down to us in a late tradition; he is the son of Persephone. If this version were not based on an old tradition, we should say that it represented a translation of the name Semele into Greek, for in the Phrygian language it signified Chthonia, the Subterranean One, that is to say, Persephone.[7]

As a parallel to the flames that consumed Semele and the funeral pyre of Koronis, on which Asklepios was born, we have here another way of expressing the state in which the miraculous birth occurred: the realm of Persephone, the underworld, the realm of the dead. And this event, the birth of a divine child in the realm of the dead, of a child of the great goddess of the underworld, a birth in death, was proclaimed by the hierophant in the Eleusinian Mysteries.

The reader will find this proclamation in Chapter V (pp. 91 f.). Though I did not set myself this aim, the studies of Asklepios here submitted converged toward this mythologem, the proclamation of the myth of a miraculous birth in death, which in the myth of healing, the myth of Asklepios, took a Hellenic turn and became a *religio medici,* the religion of the Greek physician. This free convergence is in keeping with the undogmatic style of these studies. We do not depart from this free convergence; it suffices that our findings are confirmed by the outlines of the underlying mythologem, which can be shown with precision. The fact that the name of Ariadne appears in connection with this mythologem has a chronological significance of its own. Koronis proves to be a repetition not only of Semele but also of Ariadne, for both bear dual names expressing their divine and mortal natures: Koronis was also called Aigle; Ariadne also bore the name of Aridela. This is in keeping with goddesses, probably a definite goddess, of whom we shall speak in our studies. But Ariadne as *labyrinthoio potnia,* "lady of the labyrinth," received offerings of honey in Knossos; her cult is attested in Crete in the fifteenth century and is probably the Cretan cult of the underworld goddess.[8] The story of Koronis in death bearing Apollo a son resembling him, Asklepios, may be later than the story of Ariadne, whom Dionysos made into a mother bearing in death; but it is the same pre-Hellenic sacred narrative.

∗

One reason why the authors of studies on Asklepios preferred to invent imaginary origins rather than consult the mythological traditions may be sought in chronological considerations. The temporal sequence of our mythological sources was mistaken for the chronology of the mythological contents, of the myths and the basic contexts in which they have come down to us, that is, the mythologems. But it is perfectly possible to establish a correct chronology on the basis of content.[9] An examination of its content shows that the story of Asklepios' birth is a repetition of an un-Homeric and assuredly pre-Homeric mythologem. This would scarcely have been possible at the time when the mythologem was looked upon as the special and to some extent secret possession of Eleusis on the one hand and of the Dionysian religion on the other, and was, in a manner of speaking, driven back into the special spheres of the two secret cults (for the cult of Dionysos was also a semisecret cult). At every step we shall be able to observe convergences with both these cults.

The other reason may be put down to general misgivings. In a short survey of the history of the study of myths (in his book *Theophania*, which is devoted to the spirit of the Homeric religion but by no means to the entire phenomenon of ancient Greek religion) Walter F. Otto remarked (p. 14) that the true study of myths had received its death blow in the controversy unleashed by Friedrich Creuzer's *Symbolik* (1810) and had not been revived until our own day. In a somewhat simplified form this remark characterizes the situation. Creuzer's attempt to reduce the myths to secret doctrines of the priests was so misguided that the refutation of his error led only to negation and not to any fruitful new departure. Under the false title "symbolists" the old "allegorists" had made their reappearance; these were the epigoni of the Greek Sophists, who were the first to begin reducing mythology to something else: in their case, to lessons about man and the world. Goethe, the true symbolist of 1810, rejected both Creuzer and the antisymbolist Voss. He was the only thinker to reflect seriously about symbols and to take symbolism in the sense that was actually operative in ancient religion.[10] The Aegaean scene in *Faust*, Part II, is an example of his mythology and should be considered in any science of mythology.[11] But neither his method nor his occasional remarks on symbols and allegory [12] exerted any influence on the mythologists of his own time.

Not only does Creuzer's approach to myths provide ample ground for misgiving, but also that of his successors, unless one decides to make a new beginning, to examine the material directly. Creuzer at least did not underestimate the religious significance of mythology, even though his appreciation of it was only a form of misunderstanding. But he was the first modern scholar to reduce mythology to something else, and those who came after him did essentially the same thing. They reduced it to natural phenomena, to wrong or at least peculiar ways of thinking, to poetic invention, social norms, unconscious psychic processes—always to something else, to something simple behind the richness and stratified depth of mythology, or to nothing. For one of the aims was to show that there was nothing in mythology, no meaning on which one might reflect but at most a practical purpose, a means of communicating norms, of explaining. Over and over again it was the allegorist and his adversary, the positivistic anti-allegorist and anti-symbolist who recorded the material, who, on the basis of a false chronological principle, fitted the myths into an imaginary line of development and abandoned in advance any attempt to let the mythological tradition—one ancient tradition side by side with the others—speak through an appropriate interpretation. The positivist mythologers, for their part, concentrated on negations and warnings as to what one should not look for in myths. All these fallacies resulted from false reductions, attempts to represent one special aspect of mythology as the only true and significant one.

One reason why it has been necessary to start all over from scratch is that to argue with the literature on mythology, with its fallacies and half-truths, and even to insist on those truths that have somehow been uttered leads us away from mythology itself, from concern with the tradition, and involves us in questions of theory, which though indispensable have no place in the present book.[13]

Here I should like only to recall the analogy which I took as the point of departure in my contributions to the *Essays on a Science of Mythology,* in which I strove to make a new start, unburdened by the terrifying heritage of last century's mythologers. I have in mind the analogy between mythology and music, which takes on a new depth in the light of observations which Otto has made in his book *Die Musen und der göttliche Ursprung des Singens und Sagens* ("The Muses and the Divine Origin of Singing and Speech"). By way of suggesting the view of mythology represented in the following studies on

Asklepios I should like to quote his words on music in the animal king-
dom—"primordial music" so to speak:

"Wherever a creature emits even the simplest sequence of musical
tones, it evinces a state of mind entirely different from that which occurs in the uncontrolled outcry. And this state of mind is the essential
when we ask about the nature of the primordial musicality. It is often
unmistakable that the song, even of animals, is sufficient unto itself,
that it is not intended to serve any purpose or produce any sort of ef-
fect. Such songs have aptly been characterized as self-expressions.
They arise from an intrinsic need of the creature to give expression to
its being. But self-expression demands a presence, for which it occurs.
This presence is the environing world. No creature exists for itself
alone; all are in the world, and this means: each one in its own world.
Thus the singing creature expresses itself in and for its world. In expressing itself it becomes happily aware of the world, it cries out and
joyfully lays claim to the world. The lark rises to dizzy heights in the
column of air that is its world; without other purpose, it sings the song
of itself and its world. The language of its own being is at the same
time the language of the world's reality. A living knowledge rings in
the song. When man makes music he has doubtless a much broader
and richer environment. But the phenomenon is fundamentally the
same. He too must express himself in tones, without purpose and regardless of whether or not he is heard by others. But here again self-
expression and revelation of the world are one and the same. As he
expresses himself, the reality of the being that enfolds him speaks in
his tones." [14]

Here it is the relation between self-representation and revelation of the world that I wish to take as an analogy, and *only* this relation, not the way in which it comes about. For the "primordial mythology" may well be identified with man's song of himself and his world. Mythology is man's representation of himself—in the religion of Dionysos it is actually a self-representation of the living creature—and also a revelation of the world. In mythology man's own being and the reality of the being that enfolds him are expressed simultaneously in the modality peculiar to mythology, which is not that of music or of any other art, or of philosophy or science. Nothing human, no aspect of the environing world is excluded from mythology, although in another modality the very same elements may be objects of astronomical observation or of psychological research. The only theoretical presuppositions in this book are that we cannot accept limitation to a single aspect and that we prefer the tradition to any unproved hypothesis regarding the origins.

✳

The following text springs from my study of the tradition of Asklepios between 1943 and 1947. This was an eminently philological undertaking, an attempt to interpret the sources and monuments, to go back (as I have set forth elsewhere,[15] I believe this process of "going back" to be the chief purpose of the study of classical antiquity) to the ancient world, to the immediately perceived realities of ancient existence. It is not an attempt to apply the methods of Jungian psychology. How a related theme may be treated by the Jungian school is shown by C. A. Meier's book *Antike Inkubation und moderne Psychotherapie*. Although a solid philological foundation is indispensable to all three types of study—those of Edelstein and Hausmann, that of C. A. Meier, and my own—they amount to three different approaches, which we can only hope will converge. And, indeed, in employing the word "archetypal" in the volume subtitle, as well as in the entire series of monographs of which this work is the third volume though the first to appear, I stress the possibility of convergence with modern psychology. In the English language, and in our European culture, however, the word "archetypal" is older than psychology. The English Platonists, for example, used "archetypal" for the transcendent prototypes of the realities of human existence. And wherever mythology is still alive and functioning, the same relationship prevails between mythological beings and these realities. To ancient physicians Asklepios was the prototype of their existence, the existence of the healer. In these works of mine, "existence" is not used as it is in existentialist philosophy, but in its simplest and most direct sense.

It is particularly to be hoped that Professor J. Papadimitriu's excavations, which have unearthed the temple of Apollo Maleatas above the sanctuary of Epidauros and its vast substructure with its Mycenaean vestiges, will be extended by digging in the depths of the *hieron* itself. This is our chief hope of learning more about the history of the religion of Asklepios at Epidauros. Our present picture of it is highly hypothetical.[16] A definitive proof of the sun character of Apollo, which, however, by no means excludes his other aspects, is contained in Walter F. Otto's paper "Apollon." W. Deonna [17] has written a comprehensive monograph about the little god in the hooded cloak (see our pp. 56, 58, 88). Archaeology will give further help in our attempts at "going back." It seems advisable to refrain from all hypotheses—espe-

cially that put forward by Grégoire, Goossens, and Mathieu in their
Asklèpios, Apollon Smintheus et Rudra—until the excavations have
gone deeper.

I wish to thank Ciba and Company, of Basel, for their encourage-
ment of this work, for the form in which they published it in 1947, and
for permission to use the original reproductions in the present edition.

C. K.

Casa del Sole
Ascona, Switzerland
September 1956/June 1958

Acknowledgment is gratefully made to Penguin Books Ltd. for quotations from
E. V. Rieu's translation of *The Iliad*, and to Indiana University Press for quotations from Rolfe Humphries' translation of Ovid's *Metamorphoses*.

ASKLEPIOS:

Archetypal Image of the Physician's Existence

1. *The Tiber Island in Rome before the* XIX *century. Drawing by Giovanni Battista Piranesi (*1707–78*). Note the bust of Aesculapius on the wall near the center of the picture*

I. ASKLEPIOS IN ROME

STROLLING along the Tiber in the course of a visit to Rome, we pass the Ponte Garibaldi; and then, a few steps further on, in the direction of the Aventine, we suddenly come into view of the site whence the influence of the Greek god of medicine spread through the whole Roman empire. From the Lungotevere dei Cenci we look across to the Tiber Island where the church of San Bartolomeo [1] stands amid a group of hospital buildings. Thus disposed, church and hospital are heirs to an ancient Asklepieion, a cult site unique in form.[1] On closer investigation we

3

discover, on the southern tip of the island, the remains of the old containing wall, built of travertine [2]. This wall gave the island the form of a ship [3], commemorating Asklepios' voyage from his native Epidauros to Rome. A fragment of a relief representing Asklepios—or Aesculapius, as the Romans called him—and a snake is still visible on the wall. The snake is coiled around a staff. Inside the church we find columns from an ancient temple. And we find something else that does not necessarily belong in a Christian church: the mouth of a well in the middle of the steps leading to the presbytery. The well opening is adorned with reliefs dating from the twelfth century, for the present church of San Bartolomeo was not built until close to the year 1000.

2. *Detail of the present remains of the ancient containing wall which gives the Tiber Island its shiplike form. Traces of the bust of Aesculapius and the snake-and-staff can still be seen. Nearby, one of the bulls' heads which decorated the island-ship*

The presence of a well fits in with a "temple secret" recorded by the Greek traveler Pausanias. When in the course of his visit to Epidauros he asked why no water or oil was brought to the temple to clean the ivory on the statue of Asklepios, the priests told him that there was a spring under the statue.[2] The spring was not found when the temple was excavated, but in general a spring seems to have been one of the requisites of the temples of Asklepios.

Starting from the church and hospitals on the Tiber Island, a living monument as it were to the cult of Asklepios, our road will lead us to the god in whom the physicians of antiquity saw the source and prototype of their profession, their spiritual and physical ancestor. The

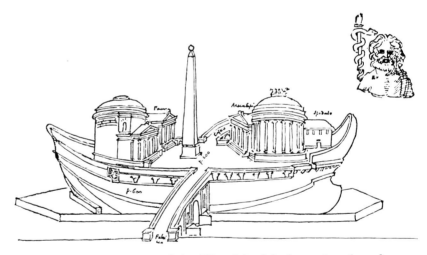

3. *Reconstruction of the Tiber Island in its ancient form by a draftsman of the* XVI *century. Upper right, the artist has reproduced the bust of Aesculapius and the snake-and-staff. The obelisk, erected in late antiquity, proves that the island-ship, turned to the west, opposite to the direction of arrival, was conceived as a sun ship*

ancient physicians took this ancestry of theirs very seriously. Classical Greek medicine flourished chiefly in Kos and Knidos in eastern Greece. Its representatives, among them Hippokrates, whom we call "the Great" to distinguish him from grandsons and other relatives bearing the same name, were members of a single family, a family of physicians. The physician's oath that has come down to us in the collection of Hippocratic writings bound everyone wishing to practice medicine to consider his teacher as his father and the teacher's sons as brothers, to whom he must impart the doctrine free of charge as though they were his own sons by blood.[3] The art of healing was handed down in a genealogical line from father to son. Paying pupils outside this line took second rank; still, they had to take the same oath, through which they became in a manner of speaking adoptive sons, members of the same great family. Asklepios was looked upon as the ancestor of the family of physicians. In their own belief the Greek physicians were descended from him and were therefore known as Asklepiadai, or "sons of Asklepios."

In connection with this living genealogy, embodied in every physician, two related facts should be considered: on the one hand a god of physicians, the Asklepios of dreams, visions, mythological and religious embodiments; on the other hand a "techne" ($\tau \acute{\epsilon} \chi \nu \eta$), a knowledge and skill handed down as a family tradition and at the same time as a hereditary talent. The cultivation of an acquired technical tradition goes hand in hand with conscious attachment to the family line. In the ancient world this attitude was reflected in a mythical genealogy and a corresponding family cult. Thus the divine author of the line is not so much the source of traditional knowledge as the supra-individual fountainhead of an inherited gift. And so we may expect the figure of

Asklepios, god of physicians, to reflect in a measure the profoundest origins of Greek medicine. Perhaps these very general remarks may lend special meaning to the historical study of an ancient god.

The arrival of Asklepios in Rome was a significant historical event; the legends surrounding it are highly instructive. They show us the god in his own atmosphere, the elements of which can be traced back to archaic Greece. In the main the sources tell the same story of how a sacred serpent was transferred from Epidauros to Rome.[4] In the years 295 and 293 B.C. the plague broke out in Rome. To the ancient mind the disease was like a fire: it was "scorching," says Livy in speaking of its devastations.[5] And in the background, behind the bodies charred by an inner fire, behind the burning heaps of corpses, the Greeks sensed the wrath of Apollo. As Homer puts it toward the beginning of the Iliad: "He shot an arrow with a dreadful twang from his silver bow, attacked the mules first and the nimble dogs; then he aimed his sharp arrows at the men, and struck again and again. Day and night innumerable fires consumed the dead."[6]

In such cases the Greeks turned to Apollo in accordance with an ancient principle of homeopathy expressed in a famous saying of the oracle of Apollo: "The wounder heals."[7] The responses given by the god when besought for his aid in combating an epidemic are recorded in inscriptions from the temple of Apollo in Klaros.[8] The oracle demanded first of all the erection of a statue of Apollo, that is to say, an embodiment of the god in the form described in the verses quoted from the Iliad. A Greek statue dating from the fourth century, a copy of which is known to us as the "Apollo Belvedere,"[9] shows us the god who kills, yet purifies and heals [4].

4. *Apollo Belvedere, perhaps interpreted in Rome as Apollo Medicus. The small snake on the tree trunk is a "friendly snake" such as might be characteristic of the god of medicine. Snake and trunk have been added by the Roman copyist*

In the year 293 the Romans consulted their own oracle of Apollo, the Sibylline Books, and were told to invite Asklepios to Rome from Epidauros. Such advice would have been inconceivable if Asklepios had not by that time been known in Italy and in Rome itself as a healer god, who in this function represented Apollo. The transfer of a powerful new god from a foreign land to Rome demanded an elaborate ceremony, to be executed with care and attentiveness—that is, *religio*.[10] At first, because the city was still at war, nothing more was done than to devote a day of prayer to Asklepios. Only in 291 were ten men, led by Quintus Ogulnius, sent to Epidauros to bring the god back to Rome. The essential features of this ceremonial event stand out clearly from Ovid's account in Book XV of his *Metamorphoses*. At the outset we encounter the belief that the cure—though indirectly—must come from Apollo. Ovid brings this out by substituting the supreme Apollonian authority, Delphi itself, for the Sibylline Books:

> Men were weary
> Of caring for the dead, and saw their efforts
> All came to nothing, found the arts of healers
> Of no avail, and so they went to Delphi,
> Earth's center, there to beg the god to help them,
> To help them in their misery, and end
> The ills of their great city. All things trembled,
> The shrine, the laurel, and Apollo's quiver,
> And from the innermost tripod came the words
> That shook them all with fear: "What you are seeking
> In Delphi, Romans, you should have sought for nearer.
> Go, seek it nearer home. Apollo cannot
> Lessen your troubles, but Apollo's son
> Has power to help you. Go, with all good omens,
> And call upon him."[11]

Thereupon the Roman Senate inquired after the abode of this son of Apollo, who was regarded as a young, still unknown god, just about to come into his inheritance. The healer god was no longer Apollo himself, who also bore the epithets "the healer" and "the physician"—to the Romans he was Apollo Medicus [12]—but Asklepios with his special cult in Epidauros. Thither emissaries were sent to bring the god himself to Rome. But the Epidaurians took a different view of the matter. To their minds Asklepios would remain forever in Epidauros but would do his work wherever, by the sending of a sacred snake, a branch of his cult was founded. Ovid describes the episode from the Roman point of view. According to him the Epidaurians were divided in their opinion: some were disinclined to withhold assistance from the Romans, others wished to keep the god for themselves. It was Asklepios himself who made the decision in his own typically Epidaurian fashion by appearing to Q. Ogulnius in a dream just as he ordinarily appeared to the sick sleeping in his temple. The god stepped up to the Roman's bedside:

> *"Be not afraid; I shall come, and leave my statues,*
> *But see this serpent, as it twines around*
> *The rod I carry: mark it well, and learn it,*
> *For I shall be this serpent, only larger,*
> *Like a celestial presence."* [13]

Asklepios appeared to Ogulnius just as he is represented in his temple, in the form recorded by the ancient sculptors. Thrasymedes had

5. *Silver coin from Epidauros, ca. 350 B.C., bearing an effigy of Asklepios. Under the throne lies a dog*

6. *The snake of the enthroned Asklepios on the Pincian Hill in Rome. The god's forearm, the snake's neck, and other parts of the statue have been restored; but the essential part, showing the snake curling round a sort of omphalos beneath the throne, dates from the II century A.D.*

fashioned him for the Epidaurians as an enthroned figure of gold and ivory, and it is thus seated, with the snake before him, that he appears on the coins of Epidauros [5]. And we have still another version of the enthroned god with the snake [6]. But at the height of his cult, attested in Epidauros by the long list of cures [14] and in Athens by Aristophanes' reference to it,[15] the patients sleeping in the temple generally dreamed of him in the form described by Ovid. It is thus that he is represented in the best-known statues [7], leaning on his staff with the snake twined round it. Ovid retains this human form of the god, though he also describes his animal manifestation.

In the morning the Epidaurians themselves asked for a sign from Asklepios:

> *And silence*
> *Had hardly fallen, when the god, all crested*
> *With gold, in serpent-form, uttered a warning,*
> *Hissed terribly, a sign that he was coming,*
> *And all the altars, all the doors, the pavement,*
> *The roof of gold, the statue, shook and trembled.*
> *Reared high, he stood there, and he gazed about him*
> *With fiery eyes, and as the people shuddered,*
> *The priest, in ceremonial headdress, knew him,*
> *Calling: "The god! Behold the god! Bow down*
> *To him in word and spirit, all who stand here!*
> *That we may see his beauty as our blessing,*
> *Here at his shrine!"* [16]

Here we have an extremely un-Greek epiphany of an otherwise beautiful Greek god! But for this very reason it offers a unique opportunity to note the characteristic feature of the religion of Asklepios that distinguishes it from the Olympian world of the Homeric gods. "Chtho-

7. *Aesculapius. From the port of Anzio, the*
Antium of antiquity, where, according to
legend, the god first landed. Roman statue.
ca. A.D. *150*

nic" would have been the ancient word for it, while today, speaking
from a different standpoint, one might say "numinous." These two
terms cover different aspects of the phenomenon, but it is in any case
the same phenomenon. D. H. Lawrence suggests the essential point
when he says that the symbol of the snake goes so deep that "a rustle
in the grass can startle the toughest 'modern' to depths he has no con-

trol over." [17] In the cult of Asklepios what is most deeply hidden in man is raised to the gold, ivory, and marble upper world of the Greek temples. This is the cult that now came to Rome. The serpent god makes his way to the harbor of Epidauros and, the narrative continues, boards the Roman ship of his own accord.

Favorable winds bear the ship to Antium. Valerius Maximus as well as Ovid relates that here the serpent left the ship to dwell in a temple. According to Ovid the temple belonged to Apollo, according to Valerius Maximus it was already dedicated to Aesculapius. But the latter tells us that the snake hung for three days from a palm tree in the outer court of the temple. This tree, not native to Italy, creates an Apollonian atmosphere. We recall the palm tree on Delos, beside which Apollo was born.[18] In a sacred grove in northern Greece snakes were kept in honor of Apollo himself and looked upon as the god's playthings.[19] *Coluber longissimus,* the species of snake sacred to Asklepios, is a tree snake which in southern climates attains a length of over six feet. A snake fancier has written of it: "I admired the elegant movements of the slender body, the shining brass-colored head, finely chiseled as the work of a goldsmith, which emitted blood-curdling hisses as it darted up and down." [20] There is nothing very dark or underworldly about a snake of this sort hanging from a tree of the sun—for such was the palm tree to the Greeks, related by its name *phoinix* to the reddish color of the sun.

We shall soon see that it makes little difference whether the temple at Antium was dedicated to Asklepios or to Apollo. The better informed of the two writers was probably Ovid, who says that there was a temple of Apollo at Antium before the arrival of Asklepios in Rome. After the god's sojourn in this temple, at all events, the ship bore him to the mouth of the Tiber. There began his solemn entry into Rome:

> . . . *and here the people*
> *Came thronging down to meet him, men and matrons*
> *And maids, the Vestals, with joyous shouts*
> *As the swift ship rode on upstream, and incense*
> *Crackled on altars on both sides the river*
> *And air was fragrant with the smoke of incense*
> *And victim beasts made the knife warm with blood.*
> *He had entered Rome, the capital of the world,*
> *And climbed the mast, and swung his head about*
> *As if to seek his proper habitation.*
> *Just at this point the river breaks and flows,*
> *A double stream, around a mole of land*
> *Men call The Island. Here the serpent-son,*
> *Apollo's offspring, came to land, put on*
> *His heavenly form again, and to the people*
> *Brought health and end of mourning.*[21]

According to the whole legendary tradition it was the snake god himself—the Phoibean,[22] i.e., Apollonian, snake as Ovid called him—who chose the Tiber Island as his abode. The scene is shown in a medal commissioned by the Emperor Antoninus Pius (A.D. 138–61) [8]. This

8. *Arrival of the Asklepios snake on the Tiber Island, where it is welcomed by Faunus, god of the island. Reverse of a bronze medal of Antoninus Pius*

choice of locality probably had profounder causes than is usually supposed. The ancients picked their cult sites on the basis of religious meanings that usually found their expression in mythology. What impelled the Romans to select this island, which could never have been healthful, for a temple and hospital dedicated to Aesculapius? The terrain was so low lying that special measures were frequently required to prevent it from becoming a morass. This state of affairs is described in the ancient sources, and Bachofen witnessed it barely a century ago.[23] Though inscriptions tell us of cures effected on the island,[24] its geographical situation makes it clear that the choice was determined by religious rather than hygienic considerations. The Tiber Island was a place of considerable religious significance: according to the Roman tradition it was originally a floating island which had formed from wheat (a plant sacred to the goddess Ceres) that had been cast into the river near the Campus Martius.[25] The relation to Mars and Ceres suggests the sphere of death and the underworld. The Campus Martius, as we know, was a burial ground. After the island had formed, it was consecrated to Faunus, the ancient Italic wolf god. For Faunus signifies "strangler," [26] and the name of his priests, the Luperci, derives plainly from *lupus,* "wolf." [27] The Romans identified Faunus with the Greek Pan, but he was wilder and had about him something of the beast of prey, expressing the wolflike quality of the all-devouring darkness. But there is an inscription that mentions not Faunus but Vediovis in connection with Aesculapius on the island: [AESCV]LAPIO VEDIOVI IN INSVLA.[28] In the early days of Rome Vediovis or Veiovis, the underworld Jupiter, took the place of the Greek Apollo who sent the plague and its cure. Not far from Rome, on Mount Soracte, the cult of this god of the underworld, named Soranus and here too identified with Apollo, was celebrated by priests who in the language of the Sabines were called *hirpi*, "wolves." [29] Soranus was connected with purifying fire: the *hirpi Sorani* leapt over the fire. Thus an Italic Apollo—an ambivalent god who killed and healed—had his place on the Tiber Island.[30] But it is in keeping with the Greek form of Apollo—the god whom we find bending his bow in the Iliad—when the Vestal Virgins invoke him as Apollo Medicus, Apollo Paean, and when a special temple of Apollo is built in order "to preserve the health of the people." [31]

As we cross over to the Tiber Island by the bridge with its ancient hermae, thinking back on the ancient Romans who brought the snake from Epidauros, we cannot help but feel a little like visitors to the underworld. Here, side by side with Faunus, the snake of Asklepios was to glitter in a wolflike nocturnal world and yet with its cold body symbolize as it were the warm light of life: a paradox that will force itself repeatedly on our attention in the course of this study. In the cult of Asklepios, as the Romans knew it on the Tiber Island, the limits between chthonic darkness and solar radiance are effaced in a way that is almost terrifying—terrifying to those who cling to the romantic conception of the Greek gods, but less so perhaps to the physician, who, even in surroundings more hygienic than the ancient temples of Asklepios on this island, is accustomed to a certain twilight realm between life and death.

II. EPIDAUROS

MOST travelers to Epidauros fail to reach the little town called Epidavros in the popular tongue. Today as in ancient times, the visitor is chiefly interested in the cult site which is still popularly termed "tò Ieró," i.e. "tò Hierón," the sanctuary. But today one no longer reaches "the arduous temple," as Ovid calls it, by way of the little harbor city, six miles below, and rarely by way of Argos, the route taken by Pausanias, the Greek globe-trotter, who toured the region in the middle of the second century A.D. Instead we take the modern highway from Navplion, present capital of the district of Argolis. For, having visited the larger and more famous excavations at Olympia in the western Peloponnese, most travelers plan only a brief stay here.

These two temples have something in common. After passing through miles of monotonous scrub, the road suddenly turns, below the village of Ligurio, into a dreamlike majestic hollow. We are already on Epidaurian soil, but still as far removed from a city as we were at Olympia. This secluded hollow is a "sacred grove" which has perhaps preserved its pristine state even more fully than the sacred precinct of Zeus Olympios, so much more open and accessible to the outside world. In both places landscape and architecture have combined to create a religious precinct centered in a valley [9]. At Olympia, where we might expect to find the abode of the Olympian ruler aloft, on a mountain or at least on a hill, it comes as a surprise to find the temple of Zeus in the plain of the Alpheios below. Such a situation seems better suited to Asklepios and his snake cult and accordingly we are far less surprised at the site chosen for the famous temple of Asklepios. The similar situations of the two sanctuaries suggest another common feature. Olympia also harbored a snake cult—in a cave at the foot of the hill of

18

9. *Topographical map of the sanctuary of Epidauros*

1 ASKLEPIEION	4 THEATER
2 GYMNASIUM	5 KATAGOGION (HOSTEL)
3 STADIUM	6 MOUNT KYNORTION

Kronos—the cult of the divine child Sosipolis, the "Savior" metamorphosed into a snake.[1]

The temple of Epidauros,[2] the foundations of which have been unearthed, was built on the model of the temple of Zeus at Olympia. The artists who adorned the temple of Asklepios with their statues represented the same stylistic trend, and apparently wished to express something common to the two deities. In both temples the enthroned statue of a solemn, bearded god is placed on a floor of black Eleusinian stone, though at Epidauros there is greater emphasis on his grave, dark aspect. Just as at Olympia, one pediment of this temple was adorned with gloomy centaurs, the only difference being that at Olympia they were to be seen on the west side, while at Epidauros the fragments of a battle of centaurs belong to the eastern pediment. The west pediment discloses a scene representing Amazons. The similarity in the decoration of the two temples and in the style of the two gods seems to suggest the same reality as the Asklepios cult at Pergamon expressed by naming its god Zeus Asklepios—a name which occurs also at Epidauros and at the neighboring city of Hermione.

If we come to Epidauros in the mood created by Olympia, we shall be reminded of the great marble head which according to some archaeologists belonged to a statue of Zeus, while others identify it as Asklepios [10].[3] The head was found in a cave on the island of Melos, once a sanctuary of Asklepios and Hygieia. The cave also contained a round base with the name of the goddess, fragments of several statuettes of Hygieia, and a votive bone dedicated to both deities. If in spite of these discoveries certain scholars have taken the colossal head of Melos for Zeus, it is because the head represents an ideal type of god deriving ultimately from Phidias's effigy of Zeus at Olympia. The most obvious marks distinguishing the statue at Epidauros from this Zeus are the snake and the dog represented beside the throne of Asklepios. Copies that have been found at Epidauros [11] give us an idea of the great dignity of the seated god. And on closer scrutiny we note a significant difference between the face of Asklepios and the head of a Zeus. What has made it definitely possible to identify the great head of Melos as Asklepios is a feature that it shares with a small votive statue found

10. *Head of Asklepios found on the island of Melos. ca. 340* B.C.

11. *Bas-relief from the sanctuary of Epidauros. It probably represents the Asklepios of the Epidaurian cult. ca. 370–360* B.C.

at Epidauros or with the head here reproduced [12], whose facial expression would not fit any other Greek god. This feature peculiar to the ideal type of Asklepios has been described as follows: The eyes seem "to look upwards and into the distance without definite aim. This combined with the vivid movement gives us an impression of a great inner emotion, one might almost say of suffering. This god does not stand be-

22

12.   *Fragment of a statue of Asklepios. ca.* 250 B.C.

fore us in Olympian calm : he is assailed as it were by the sufferings of men, which it is his vocation to assuage." [4] We have, to be sure, no reason to suppose that the oldest seated statue of Asklepios disclosed such emotion: it seems preferable to attribute the note of pathos to Skopas rather than to Thrasymedes, creator of the enthroned figure at Epidauros. But ever since this ideal of Asklepios was established, a gentle god, friendly to man, seems to have presided over the sacred valley.

Who then was the lord of this mountain and forest sanctuary, the mysterious god whose classical form stood in so noteworthy a relation to the figure of Zeus? His temple—as we can still see by the foundations [13]—stands within a walled oblong enclosure, but like most of the Greek temples not in its center [14]. What distinguished this sacred enclosure from most of the temple grounds known to us was the great peristyle of double columns on the north side, the western wing of which was composed of two stories.[5] The peristyle was designed for the patients who came to sleep in the sanctuary; whether it was the actual place of "incubation" is uncertain. The inner wall was adorned with countless votive tablets. Here too were engraved the official lists of cures,[6] six tablets of which were still in place when Pausanias visited Epidauros, and three of which were found in the course of the excavations. The first tablet begins with an invocation of "God" and "good fortune." Then come the words: "Cures of Apollo and Asklepios."[7] This does not seem to fit in with the reports of travelers, in which only Asklepios and never Apollo is named. Hence we must ask: Who was the actual god, Apollo or Asklepios?

The cures recorded in the tablets also represent an enigma, though of a more general kind. They raise the same problem as most of the "miraculous cures" at the many Christian places of pilgrimage in southern and central Europe. They are "miraculous" only insofar as *every* cure, every happy end to a situation implying the possibility of an unhappy one, is a kind of miracle. Wherever a living creature—who might equally well be called a dying creature—is gravely ill, every turn for the better involves an element of mystery, even when the physician has recognized and eliminated the cause of sickness. For the

13. *Southeasterly view from the sanctuary of Epidauros toward Mount Kynortion. This is probably the panorama that could be seen from the great hall of the Asklepieion, except that in antiquity the mountains were densely wooded*

14. *Plan of the sanctuary of Epidauros*

    1 TEMPLE OF ASKLEPIOS   4 PERISTYLE
    2 THOLOS   5 BATHS
    3 GREAT ALTAR   6 TEMPLE OF ARTEMIS

N
↑

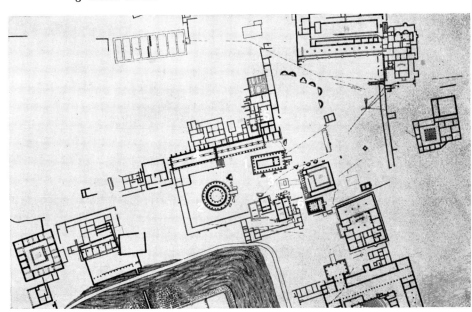

physician cannot act alone; side by side with his outside intervention something inside the patient must lend a helping hand if a cure is to be accomplished.[8] At the crucial moment something is at work that might best be compared to the flow of a spring. Popular Christian belief attributes this event to the intercession of a saint, of one especially favored by divine grace. According to this faith the basic reason for the cure is God, although he is not specifically a healer; if he so wills, he can induce anything and everything to take a turn for the better. In any case the saint only *assists*. The significance of a god specifically characterized as a god of healing is that he, in a manner of speaking, is the fountainhead. He not only assists at the turn for the better; his manifestation is the cure, or, to put it the other way round, every cure is his epiphany.

Thus the cures at Epidauros are no more mysterious than the cures effected anywhere else; healing itself is the mystery. But at Epidauros we face a special riddle: who is the god whose epiphany signifies cure? So far we have spoken only of Asklepios or of Zeus Asklepios, though in Rome we mentioned a wolf Apollo and an underworld Jupiter, Veiovis, closely related to Aesculapius. How did the Greeks view the god of healing and what did they call him? When the priests of the temple invoked the "god," they meant both Apollo and Asklepios: both were named in the lists of cures, but only Asklepios as the healer. In view of the sanctity of the place, this cannot be imputed to carelessness or chance or a desire to curry favor with Apollo.[9] As the greater of the two gods, Apollo had no need to assert his rights in a sanctuary that belonged in a very special way to his son Asklepios. He had so many holy places in Greece. And in a sense the very surroundings made Epidauros one of these. We have compared it with Olympia; but certain of its features recall the most famous of all the sites sacred to Apollo.

The temple at Delphi was built in a wild ravine, allegedly over a cleft in the rock. The spring of Kassotis flows through the foundations of the temple. At Epidauros Pausanias heard of a spring under the statue of the god. Since the excavators did not find it, the water must have been channeled in from outside. Abundance of water, free-flowing fountains were essential to the life and atmosphere of this sanctuary. Water for the Greeks was a kind of communication with the depths of the earth. And since in ancient times the traveler usually came to the sanctuary from the port of Epidauros by way of the ravine, he came into contact (very much as on the road to Delphi from its port) with something far more underworldly than at Olympia . . .

At Epidauros Apollo bore the epithet Maleatas and was worshiped in a separate little sanctuary on Mount Kynortion in the southeast corner of the hollow. The name Kynortion is connected with the Greek words for "dog" and "ascent." As the serpent ruled in the valley, up here on the mountain the dog seems to have reigned. But Apollo was also represented down in the valley. The poems of Isyllos,[10] an Epidaurian of the fourth century, engraved in stone, tell us that a certain Malos was first to build an altar and offer up a sacrifice to Apollo Maleatas. This altar apparently stood at the entrance to the great sanctuary, for Isyllos adds that at Trikka also, the most celebrated of the Thessalian temples of Asklepios, sacrifices were first offered to Apollo. Thus Apollo came first in the cult: in mythological terms, he was the "father." In another version, transmitted by Pausanias,[11] Phlegyas, a warlike king from Thessaly, and his daughter, Apollo's beloved, come to Epidauros when she is near to childbirth. Here she abandons the child Asklepios on a mountain, then known as the Mount of Myrtles, later on the Mountain of the Teats. There the shepherd Aresthanas finds the child lying between a goat and a dog: the goat suckles the child and the dog guards him, all in a light so dazzling that the shepherd has to turn away as from a divine epiphany. At the same moment a voice is heard, proclaiming over land and sea that the newborn babe will discover every cure for the sick and awaken the dead. In his hymn in honor of Apollo and Asklepios, Isyllos also transfers the story of the divine birth to Epidauros, but his narrative is richer in mythological details and allusions which, though they solve the enigma of father and son, leave us with the problem of the mother.

In this version Malos, a primeval man whom Zeus has united in sacred marriage with an Apollonian virgin, the Muse Erato, begets a daughter, Cleophema, "Proclaimer of Glory," another Muselike figure. At this point in the story we encounter the words: "And by Phlegyas was begotten—and her name was Aigla—this was her second name— but at that time she was generally called Koronis." [12] In speaking of the future bride of Apollo, Isyllos stammers intentionally, because he is not allowed to utter her true name. Koronis could only be a dark-haired, dark-skinned maiden, for the name Koronis evokes the Greek word for "crow." [13] But she is also called Aigla, the "Luminous One," identical with the Greek word for "light" and "radiance." And the child she has borne in the sanctuary is "by Apollo surnamed Asklepios after his mother Aigla." [14] Indeed, name and surname are related; the transitional forms have been found, and strange as the phonetic change may seem, it must be acknowledged. [15] The irregularity may be explained by the influence of a pre-Hellenic, archaic Mediterranean language. Certain of Apollo's surnames are derived from αἴγλη. On the isle of Anaphe, which takes its name from a word meaning "to kindle," Apollo Aigletes, the Luminous Apollo, "shone" like a beacon before the Argonauts. On Anaphe itself "Aigletes" was "Asgelatas," to which "Asklepios" is phonetically related. In regard to meaning it can also be equated with "Aiglaeis" and "Aglaopes," self-evident designations of luminous beings. For Isyllos, who took his religion seriously, "Asklepios" was only the god's "surname," his *epiklesis*. For him the surname had the same meaning as Pausanias's story of the divine child's light-epiphany. According to these mythologems Asklepios is the procreative Apollo, flaring up from out of a mother both dark and bright. The close connection between Apollo and Asklepios attested by so many inscriptions at Epidauros [16] can be traced back to the unity of the greater god (Apollo) with one of his aspects (Asklepios), a unity that was long preserved on the isle of Anaphe in the form Apollo Aigletes or Apollo Asgelatas.

The effulgent Apollo, the Apollo who flares up, appears at Epidauros as Asklepios. Here we must not think solely of an outward manifestation of light, the sunrise. True, it is no accident that Apollo Maleatas was worshiped on an eminence dominating the eastern end of the valley and that here on the heights the child Asklepios shone like the rising sun. The dog, the animal that gave its name to Mount Kynortion, can also be golden in Greek mythology.[17] The wolf, related to the dog but identified with darkness, was sacred to Apollo, whom we have encountered in Italy as a wolf god, to whom wolves were actually sacrificed at Argos,[18] and upon whose altar at Delphi stood a bronze wolf in the guise of an offering.[19] As compared to Maleatas, Asklepios—guarded as a child by

15. *Votive relief from Epidauros. From right to left, it represents Asklepios, his two sons Machaon and Podaleirios (accompanied by dogs), three goddesses, and at the far right two worshipers. ca. 360 B.C.*

a dog, god of healing accompanied by dogs [15]—seems to represent another, more luminous aspect of Apollo. In general we may say that in mythology the "father" is always "darker" than the "son." "Maleatas" signifies "he who is from Malea," and Malea, the name of a headland on the southern Peloponnese, is associated with equine or goatlike procreator gods: with Poseidon, Chiron, Silenos.[20] The paternal aspect of Apollo discloses a kinship with such beings—but only his paternal aspect. In a list of gods found in one of the temples of Asklepios,[21] Maleatas is mentioned *before* Apollo as a separate god, as though the author wished to avoid mentioning Apollo under this dark name. In Zeus Asklepios we discern this "father," not the Olympian but the underworld Zeus: a shade of darkness mingled with the brightest effulgence, a gentle grav-

ity, pertaining not to the real sunrise but to the god who appears in the
nightly dreams of the sick.

And like the real sunrise, real birth and real death (and what is
thought to follow death, the resurrection of the dead) have no part in
the divine events that took place in the dark night at the temple of
Epidauros. According to Isyllos, the birthplace of Asklepios was the
temple itself. But in this place of healing only a divine birth, only an
epiphany of the god of healing, could occur. Women in labor were excluded from the sacred precinct, for pregnancy is not an ailment that
calls for cure. Nor could the dying be taken into the sanctuary. It was
only in the days of the Roman emperors, when healing had lost its meaning as a divine event and Epidauros had become a kind of climatic resort
and sanitarium in the broadest sense of the word, that halls for ex-
pectant mothers and the dying were built outside the sanctuary. Nowhere in the records of cures, which include so many "miracles," is
there any mention of the raising of the dead foreseen in the above-
mentioned account of the birth of Asklepios. The myth, it is true, tells us
of resurrections effected by Asklepios and also of his own death, inflicted on him as punishment for them.[21a] But not a single legend relating
to resurrection or to the god's death has been found recorded at Epidauros. Actually there is no mention of anyone's death, for it would have
been absurd to include cases where no epiphany occurred in a record of
epiphanies. However, if the resurrection of a dead man had been regarded as appropriate at Epidauros, it would have been easy to invent
one.

The turn for the better is no actual sunrise, but only a kind of sunrise; it is not the actual birth of a man and not the resurrection of the

dead, but an event enacted as it were on the borders of the realm of the dead. Underworldly when it accompanies Hekate, the dog also suggests the rising of the light; here evidently it designates a transitional situation: the transition between below and above, night and day, death and life. And the more familiar of the animals sacred to Asklepios, the snake, marks the same situation. There is a striking equivalence of dog and snake in the Greek mythology of the underworld; their forms merge and their meanings as well. "Dogs," says an ancient exegete, "are also snakes." [22] The equation can only be taken to mean that both animals may express the same psychic content. At first an animal symbol had meaning only in the geographical habitat of the animal in question. But when a people migrated, it took along its domesticated animals and its memories of the fauna of its former home. Thus after the Greeks had settled in a country rich in snakes they continued to favor the dog as a symbol side by side with the snake. We have here the same phenomenon as the appearance of the he-goat in the cult of the Roman wolf priests, the Luperci,[23] or the alternation of bear and lion in the cults and myths of the goddess Artemis.

Dog and snake, these symbols [24] offered by nature itself, express the same situation, the turn for the better at the brink of the underworld, and in the Epidaurian records they appear in the same function. "A dog has cured a boy from Aigina," says an inscription.[25] "He had a growth on his neck. When he came to the god, one of the sacred dogs treated him with its tongue (the boy was awake) and made him well." In another report [26] the healer is a snake: "A man's toe was cured by a snake. This man was very ill with a malignant abscess of the toe. By day he was taken outside by servants and made to sit in a chair. When sleep over-

16. *Votive relief from the Asklepieion at Athens. A family sacrifices to Asklepios: in the background, the goddess Hygieia and a serpent descending a tree of the sacred grove; on the altar, fruit and cakes. ca. 330 B.C.*

took him, a snake came from the innermost chamber of the sanctuary, cured his toe with its tongue, and having done so withdrew. When he woke up healed, he said he had beheld a vision; he had dreamed that a comely youth had applied a salve to his toe."

These tales of miracles with their sharp distinction between dream and waking are presented as "true stories" of events that have taken place in the sanctuary. Some of them might indeed be true accounts of actual happenings. This account, for instance, of the cure of a mute girl: "While running about in the sanctuary, she saw a snake creeping down from one of the trees in the grove [16]. Terrified, she cried out for her mother and father; then she went away, cured." [27] But on the whole these stories about animals should be interpreted as dreams. The sacred animals symbolize life at the threshold of death, a hidden force, dark and cold, but at the same time warm and radiant, that stirs beneath the surface of the waking world and accomplishes the miracle of cure. The vision of the beautiful young healer appearing while the patient's toe is being cured by the snake is a kind of dream within a dream, an amplification reaching out for a still deeper meaning—the immediate experience of the divine in the natural miracle of healing.

The purpose of a visit to the sanctuary of Epidauros was to meet this divine power halfway. This was no visit to a doctor who simply administers medicine; it was an encounter with the naked and immediate event of healing itself, experienced sometimes in sublime [17] and

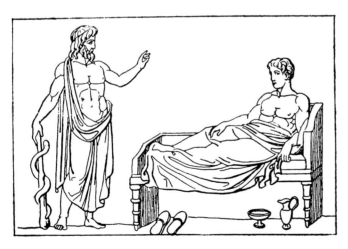

17. *Drawing after a votive relief now lost: Asklepios appearing to a sick man. The raised left arm expresses the god's personal relation to the patient*

sometimes in more realistic visions [18]. In many of these dreams the
god intervened directly. Pamphaes of Epidauros was afflicted with a
"festering abscess in the mouth. Sleeping in the innermost chamber of
the sanctuary, this man beheld a vision: he dreamed that the god
opened his mouth, held his jaws apart with a wedge, and cleansed the
mouth. Thereupon he became well." [28] Characteristically, this cure is
sought in sleep and dreams. In sleep the patient withdraws from his
fellow men and even from his physician, and surrenders to a process at
work within him. When the votive reliefs show other human beings
present at the cure—devout, awestruck relatives or assistants such as
might attend an ordinary operation—the outward aspect of the process
is merely being represented in one with the religious experience.

The sufferer who came to the Asklepieion observed a cult, but we
know little about the details of its practice at Epidauros. We do not

18. *Votive relief dedicated to Asklepios, from the Asklepieion
of Piraeus. The god is shown treating a patient. Behind
Asklepios, Hygieia. Left, members of the patient's family.
ca. 400 B.C.*

know the situation of the abaton, the "innermost chamber" of the sanctuary to which the patient withdrew for the temple sleep, the *incubatio*. Snakes were encountered at every step. The priests were certainly not without medical training or ability. But their role, aside from deciding whom to admit, seems to have been largely passive. The dying, as we have said, were excluded and the rest were shrewdly left to their own "process of healing." This process was so much like the usual incubation practiced at the oracle sites that some persons came to Epidauros in search not of healing but of the god's advice in difficulties unrelated to

19. *Votive relief of Archinos dedicated to the oracle god Amphiaraos at Oropos (Attica). In the foreground, the invalid dreams that the god is performing an operation on him. But in the background we see that the patient is being licked by a snake. ca. 380–370 B.C.*

20.   *Asklepios in the form of a wandering
youth. ca.* A.D. *140*

21. *Votive relief dedicated to Asklepios. A man and a boy offer up*
a pig—the usual sacrifice to chthonic deities—to the enthroned
god and Hygieia. ca. 300 B.C.

health. Conversely, an oracle god such as Amphiaraos at the Attic shrine
of Oropos sometimes acted as a physician [19]. But unlike the oracles,
the cult at Epidauros created in its devotees the expectation of a great

38

22. *Initiation rites represented in relief on the so-called Lovatelli Urn: probably the lesser mysteries of Agrai, which were a preparation for the great Mysteries of Eleusis. The initiate (Herakles) appears in several successive situations: right to left, sacrificing a pig, veiled, and finally playing with the snake of the goddess of the underworld. From the Esquiline. Early II century A.D.*

culminating experience. In this essential point Epidauros comes close to Eleusis. Indeed Epidauros and Eleusis had more in common than the general character of mystery common to both temples. It is not very significant in itself that at later times "hierophants," Eleusinian priests, played a part at Epidauros.[29] But there must have been some good reason for it if, after the cult of Asklepios had been introduced in Athens, the *Epidauria*, the "Epidaurian rites," were incorporated in the Eleusinian Mysteries. Little as we know of the rites of Epidauros and Eleusis, their mythological expressions are known to us and show significant parallels.

Asklepios no doubt appeared to his worshipers in different forms— the Apollonian youth [20] is just as worthy of our attention as the enthroned Zeuslike man [21]—but his epiphany as experienced in the cult was the flaring-up of a divine child, which was greeted with loud cries. "To him I cry, the beautiful child and great light of man, Asklepios," says the chorus in Aristophanes when Ploutos, the blind god of riches, opened his eyes in the Asklepieion of Piraeus.[30] The birth of a divine child was experienced and proclaimed in the same form in the final act of the Eleusinian Mysteries.[31] And just as Isyllos of Epidauros links this luminous birth with a mysterious mother, whose surnames he lists without revealing her actual name, the holy mother of the Eleusinian child is also looked upon as unnamable.[32] Emerging from the darkness that shrouded him at the beginning of his initiation,[33] the initiate advances toward the throne of the ineffable goddess and is received by a friendly snake [22]. Here the imagery of the underworld plays a far greater role than at Epidauros, but as at Epidauros the underworld is not experienced as a realm of the dead, from which no return, no rebirth, is possible. The rites of Eleusis lead us to still greater depths than those of Epidauros. The way was the same, but the sick man who

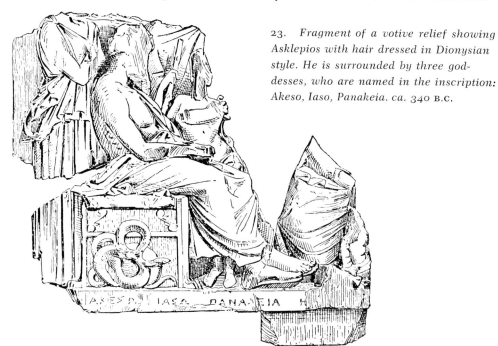

23. *Fragment of a votive relief showing Asklepios with hair dressed in Dionysian style. He is surrounded by three goddesses, who are named in the inscription: Akeso, Iaso, Panakeia. ca.* 340 B.C.

found health at Epidauros turned back sooner than the Eleusinian initiate who made his way to the Queen of the Underworld.

At Eleusis the great goddess disclosed the mystery of immortality: she was mother and daughter in one, woman bearing herself forever anew.[34] At Epidauros the male principle predominated, flaring up in the fullness of its power and bursting through the darkness. Barren women came to Epidauros to be impregnated by the god. "Nikesibule of Messene," says one of the records,[35] "slept in the sanctuary in order to be favored with progeny and beheld a dream. She dreamed that the god had come to her, followed by a snake with which she copulated. And within a year she gave birth to two boys." Because his mother had undergone a similar experience Aratos, the great soldier and statesman of Sikyon (third century B.C.), was looked upon as the son of Asklepios.[36] The snake was the form of the god's epiphany. In another report,[37] concerning Queen Andromache of Epirus, the god himself appears in the same function: "She slept in the inner chamber of the sanctuary and beheld a dream: she dreamed that a beautiful boy uncovered her, whereupon the god touched her with his hand." Andromache then conceived a son by her husband Arybbas, king of Epirus.

In the picture of the sanctuary of Epidauros, which is still far from having disclosed to us all its secrets, another feature is notable: the face of Asklepios. Grave, virile, cognizant of human suffering, it is by no means lacking in spirit. But the annihilating Apollonian sharpness of this spirit is attenuated by a darker warmth suggesting a kinship with Dionysos. This kinship is discernible in a relief representing a pre-classical Asklepios [23]. No doubt there was more than one reason for building the Asklepieion at Athens near the precinct consecrated to

24A. *View of the Asklepieion at Athens on the southern slope of the Akropolis. Above, the retaining wall of the Akropolis and a section of the sacred enclosure of Dionysos with choragic monuments (victory columns)*

24B. *Another view of the Asklepieion at Athens*

Dionysos on the southern slope of the Akropolis [24]. Nor is the Dionysian element entirely lacking in the sanctuary of Epidauros. In the western half of the sacred enclosure there stand the foundations of a puzzling rotunda, which seems in a way to symbolize the mysterious aspect of this whole sanctuary [25]. These foundations form a typical labyrinth of concentric circles, so connected by openings that in order to reach the center from the outermost ring one must fully describe each and every circle. The superstructure consisted of a circular wall between two colonnades, with an entrance from the east surmounted by a richly ornamented architrave. The outside of the building was painted in bright colors, while on the inside the base of the circular wall was of black marble. The inner walls [26] were also adorned with paintings. Pausanias was especially struck by two figures: a divine child whom, in accordance with the conventions of his time, he interpreted as an

43

Eros who has forsaken bow and arrow for the lyre and a woman drinking from a transparent glass vessel whom Pausanias calls Methe, "Drunkenness." [38] This without doubt was a Dionysian figure, who like the child bore a relation to the cult for which this building served.

Pausanias calls the circular edifice *thymele* (a kind of altar), a word that designates the most important place in the Dionysian theater. In the scholarly literature on Epidauros it is called the *tholos*, or rotunda. The excavator who discovered it regarded it as a place for mystery rites. [39] Even today nothing more definite can be said of it. [40] All we know is that even at a later date a semisubterranean rotunda was still connected with the cult of Asklepios, as has been shown by the excavation of the Asklepieion at Pergamon [27], the largest and most famous in Asia Minor. The author of these lines climbed down into the labyrinth

25. *The labyrinthine substructure of the tholos of Epidauros in its present state*

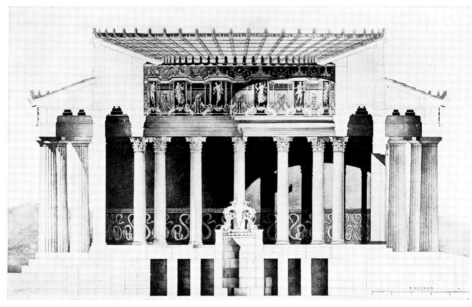

26.   *Cross section of the reconstructed tholos*

27.   *The Asklepieion of Pergamon. Model as reconstructed by H. Schleif.
The rotunda corresponding to the tholos of Epidauros is visible in
the foreground*

of the tholos at Epidauros and among the marble fragments found a piece of sculpture representing a tree trunk with a mouse or rat sitting on it: an allusion to Apollo Smintheus, the god who sent mice and the plague.[41] The surname Smintheus, borne by Apollo in the Iliad where he sends the plague, comes from *sminthos,* a Greek and probably pre-Hellenic word for mouse. But Apollo is also the only god possessing the attributes of the bow and the lyre.[42] Regardless of the Dionysian accessories that accompanied this birth of a divine child, it was a rebirth in the sense that one aspect of Apollo emerged in place of another; a power that killed was transformed into a power of healing. And this, essentially, is what the sick sought at Epidauros.

III. THE SONS OF ASKLEPIOS ON KOS

THE DODECANESE island of Kos has never been included in the usual itinerary of travelers; it seems to sleep as though under a gentle spell. But this has made it all the more attractive to archaeologists, who have taken particular interest in the Asklepieion, discovered in 1902 and excavated in the following years.[1] It has held numerous surprises; some of its secrets have not yet been divulged and we still have much to learn from it. There is nothing unusual about the site itself. In contrast to what we have observed in Rome, the Greeks, according to the ancient writers, selected healthful sites, rich in springs, for their temples of Asklepios.[2] The proximity of other gods and cults had something to do with the choice, but undoubtedly climatic conditions were also taken into consideration. The sanctuaries of both Athens and Epidauros are blessed with good clean air and both are sheltered from the wind. The same was to be expected at Kos, an ancient center of medical science, and it was no surprise when the foundations of the great Asklepieion were discovered a few miles inland from the city of Kos, on a gentle, healthful rise of ground not far from a mineral spring [28].

What did seem surprising was the chronology of this Asklepieion. Something had been known of this sanctuary and the works of art it contained ever since 1891, when the newly discovered *Mimiamboi* of the Koan poet Herondas (who lived about 250 B.C.) were published. The fourth poem, entitled "Women offering sacrifices in the temple of Asklepios," describes two simple women of Kos on their early morning pilgrimage to the sanctuary.[3] It takes us into a Greek temple of the third century B.C., into an atmosphere of popular religion transfigured by a naïve enjoyment of art. The excavations show—and this is where the

28. *View from the upper terrace of the Asklepieion at Kos. In the foreground are the ruins of the great temple of the* II *century* B.C. *In antiquity the region was wooded*

surprise came in—that at Herondas's time this temple had just been built and that the statues at which the two women marveled were then new. Herondas, a contemporary of the great Alexandrians and of Theokritos with whom as a poet he had much in common, sang the new glory of Kos, the fame of its Asklepieion, *after* its ancient glory had been secured for all time by Hippokrates and his school of medicine.

Until then we had taken a different view of the relation between Hippokrates and the Asklepieion. The belief that Hippokrates derived his science from the temple's reports of cures has come down to us from antiquity.[4] The women in the poem of Herondas present a votive tablet with a report of this kind. But the excavations have shown that this custom was developed very late at Kos, and on a very small scale in comparison to Epidauros; they also show that for chronological reasons

48

29.   *Middle terrace of the Asklepieion of Kos. In the foreground, the remains of the great altar. In the background, ruins of the small and most ancient temple*

these tablets cannot be regarded as the source of Koan medicine. A vast compound grew up above and below the little temple visited by the women [29]; in particular, a far larger temple was built on the upper terrace in the second century B.C. Today we can reconstruct this immense sanitarium with its temples and halls from the remains that have been found [30]. It has very little to do with the traditions of the ancient Koan religion of Asklepios but bears witness rather to the influence of Epidauros. If we wish to learn something about the religion of Asklepios as embodied in the Koan physicians before they submitted to the influence of Epidauros, we must look into the conditions prevailing at Kos before the Asklepieion was built.

An Asklepieion constructed on the Epidaurian model and utilized

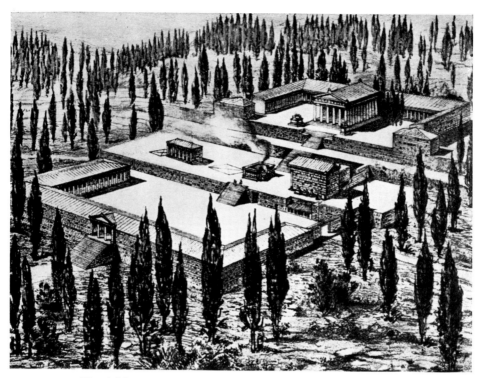

30. *The Asklepieion of Kos in Hellenistic times. Reconstruction*

as a place for "incubation" served for the most direct possible method of healing. The patient himself was offered an opportunity to bring about the cure whose elements he bore within himself. To this end an environment was created which, as in modern spas and health resorts, was as far as possible removed from the disturbing and unhealthful elements of the outside world. The religious atmosphere also helped man's innermost depths to accomplish their curative potentialities. In principle the physician was excluded from the individual mystery of recovery: the patient sought out the deity in a much more personal way than in the great mysteries of the archaic or classical period. It is therefore to be presumed that at Epidauros the physician remained intentionally in the background. To what extent this was true on the island of Kos, which had become famous for its medical school, is not known. It is quite possible that the increased medico-scientific influence that later made itself felt in most Asklepieia emanated from Kos. The line of historical development is probably as follows: first the school of physicians at Kos achieved a high level of medical science; next a turn toward religious depth, originating at Epidauros, spread to Kos itself; finally, in the early imperial age, the medical element regained its predominance, even at Epidauros. The pre-Epidaurian period at Kos was not necessarily irreligious; it was merely characterized by a different kind of religion—a religion not of the patient but of the physician, who accordingly played the leading role.

When medical science was at its height at Kos, there was no temple of Asklepios but rather a state hospital, where citizens received medical treatment free of charge. One is amazed to learn how far back this state medical assistance reaches. Charondas, the semilegendary lawgiver of the Greek city of Katana in Sicily, to whom the Koans attributed certain of their institutions, is said to have found a system of public medical assistance already in existence.[5] The legislation attributed to Charondas grew up in a region where Greek medicine had flourished in a definitely religious setting. This setting was provided by Pythagoreanism with its characteristic Apollonian religion, which included the doctrine of a purely spiritual god embodied in human form, eminently in that of Pythagoras.[6] A younger contemporary of the Apollonian sage was the outstanding physician Alkmaion.[7] Nowhere would a "nationalized" form of medicine on selflessly spiritual, religious foundations seem more natural than among the Pythagoreans of southern Italy. And without such a religious background it would scarcely have been conceivable in the ancient world.

At Kos this background may be sought in the family cult of the Asklepiads, whose moral postulates are known to us from the oath of the Greek physicians. The name of Asklepiads is to be taken literally: according to their tradition, which we mentioned at the beginning of our study, they were descendants of Apollo's son Asklepios, whose knowledge and essence they transmitted to their own sons. The genealogy of this family—one of the foremost among the Koan aristocracy—reaches back to archaic Thessaly and to times preceding the island's colonization by the Greeks.[8] Whether the line passed through Argolis and Epidauros, as seems possible in view of a remark in Herodotos,[9] or whether the founders and priests of the Epidaurian sanctuary belonged to a branch of this line, is hard to determine. In any event, this family's special gift took a different form at Kos from that of Epidauros. It expressed itself in an active intellectual concern with practical science rather than in a passive, mystical, and visionary vein. But this does not mean that the Koan form was any less religious than the Epidaurian. For to the ancient mind an attitude of reverence toward the origin of any mode of existence—in this case the origin of the medical profession and of the physician's existence—is religious.

One of the letters [10] attributed to the great Hippokrates tells us, rather in the style of a short story, of a celebration that seems to have been the special festival of the Asklepiads at Kos. This festival, called the Lifting of the Staff,[11] was connected with an annual pilgrimage to the sacred cypress grove not far from the city of Kos. It is not said that the "staff" is a branch from the grove, but this seems highly probable. A cypress branch will scarcely yield a very straight staff, and the one borne by a very realistic statue from Rhodes [31] might easily have

31. *Statuette of Asklepios from Rhodes. It represents the ideal of Asklepios in the humanized form of Hellenistic times. ca.* A.D. *140*

32. *Fragment of a bas-relief from the Asklepieion at Athens. Below, the snake-and-staff of the god. With his right hand the god is administering medicine to a patient.* IV *century* B.C.

been taken from a cypress grove. It does not differ essentially from a Greek king's scepter, which is nothing other than a staff that was handed down from generation to generation in noble—in Homeric times royal—families.[12] The snake twined round the staff of Asklepios [32] is a second attribute whose symbolism, pointing to the origin of the family in question, coincides with that of the staff itself. The ceremony of lifting this staff and bringing it back to the sacred grove was a symbolic return of the family to its origin, to Asklepios and Apollo. This clear, simple ritual takes on rich meaning when we consider the relation between Apollo and the cypress.

Not far from the city of Kos there was a cypress grove dedicated to Apollo Kyparissios. This can only have been the grove where shortly after the death of Hippokrates the first Koan temple of Asklepios and later the entire Asklepieion were built. There can be no doubt as to which of his aspects Apollo disclosed in a cypress grove. In the Mediterranean countries the relation between the world of the tombs and this dark tree with its everlasting green and its masculine upward-striving power, bearing witness to indestructible life, has remained unchanged from antiquity to our own day.[13] And it is not without significance that the statue of the Roman Veiovis, who had the attributes of a dark Apollo and was worshiped on the Tiber Island in close association with Aesculapius, was carved of cypress wood.[14] According to the legend, the cypress was originally a beautiful youth, named Kyparissos, Apollo's favorite. This youth killed his pet stag by mistake and, consumed by grief, was ultimately transformed into a tree. This legend, which has come down to us only in a late, Hellenistic version, was believed to have originated on the island of Keos, not Kos.[15] In addition to naming Apollo, it alludes to him in two ways: through the cypress and through the stag, which is an attribute of Apollo scarcely less than of his sister Artemis.[16] Both cypress and stag appear in a close mythological connection with the Asklepiads of Kos; indeed it would not be inappropriate to speak of them as the totem plant and the totem animal of the family that celebrated its festival in the cypress grove. According to the legend, one of the ancestors of Hippokrates was named Nebros, "the young stag." [17] Consulted about the plague that was raging in Delphi, the oracle enjoined the suppliants to seek the aid of the "stag's son" and the "golden one." These epithets were interpreted as referring to Nebros the Koan physician and his son Chrysos, who were duly called to Delphi. When Chrysos fell in battle with the inhabitants of Krisa, he was buried in the hippodrome. His name, signifying "gold," and the fact that he was buried on the site of the ritual chariot races, whose relation to the course of the sun is clear,[18] show that this son of Nebros is a small sun and that he, that is the stag, is the dark animal father of the luminous sun.

These mythological traits of the legend of Nebros belong to a family tradition that the Asklepiads brought with them from the north, from Thessaly. The name "Nebros, son of Nebros," occurs in Koan inscriptions,[19] bearing witness to the profound relation with the mythological animal that has led us to speak of it as a "totem animal"; still, since there was no totemic social structure in Greece, it would be more accurate to call it a "symbolic animal." In addition to this northern "symbolic animal," the family adopted the southern cypress as a "symbolic plant" expressing the same consciousness of the divinity of the family and its members. In the days of the great Hippokrates (died about 377 B.C.), when Epidauros was at the height of its glory, the name of Drako, "the

snake," also made its appearance in the family. This name was said to
have been given to the second son of Hippokrates and to a son of his
first son Thessalos, the "Thessalian." [20] It is obviously on Kos that we
must place the beginnings of the family's new "symbolic animal" which,
in combination with the staff of this noble line descended from the gods,
provided the insignia of the medical profession. At that time the first
temple of Asklepios was built in the grove of Apollo Kyparissios. It was
gradually enlarged to form a sanitarium, and the mysterious source of
healing which the Koan physicians cultivated as a family heritage was
made accessible to the sick along the lines laid down at Epidauros.

An altar for Asklepios, set up toward the middle of the fourth century B.C., before the building of the first temple, was adorned with
symbols more meaningful than the animal and plant symbols that had
long since become mere conventions. Along with Machaon, the son of
Asklepios, Helios and Hemera, "Sun" and "Day," were worshiped here. [21]
Hekate, the moon goddess, was also remembered. Outstanding among
the remaining female companions of Asklepios were Epione, held to be
his wife, and Hygieia, regarded as his daughter. Later on, Hygieia came
to be represented as his divine companion and feminine counterpart
[33 and 34]. Hemera, goddess of day, is mentioned with Asklepios only
on this altar; Helios appears with him more frequently, and in the inscriptions his name precedes that of Asklepios. [22] This in itself makes it
clear that he is no secondary figure. To be sure, the wisdom of the ancient physicians and of those who conceived the temples ascribed the
mysterious process of healing rather to the night and sleep than to the
day and waking. One indication of this is the institution of the "temple
sleep." Another is a dwarflike, nocturnal figure, a child in a hooded cloak

33. *Statuette of Hygieia from Rhodes.*
It shows the close connection between the
goddess and the snake. ca. A.D. *140*

34. *Late Roman ivory carving*
representing Hygieia. Her snake is
Apollonian: it emerges from a tripod.
Above, ritual utensils suggesting the
mysteries: right, wine pitcher with snake
and, left, storage basket—the cista
mystica—*also with snake and a divine*
child. Below, near the goddess, another
version of the divine child. End of the IV
century A.D.

who often appears as a companion of Asklepios and who, on the strength of an oracle, was worshiped in the Asklepieion of Pergamon.[23] Here the little god bore the ambiguous name Telesphoros, meaning "the Finisher," for death too is a finisher—but elsewhere he was known as Akesis, "healing." [24] We shall come back to him in the last chapter of this book. The nocturnal background was already present in the cypress grove of the dark Apollo, who provided the model for the Roman Veiovis. And here, represented side by side with Asklepios, Sun and Day also have a dark background; for in both logic and experience every light stands against a dark background. We shall see their religious significance in the cult of Asklepios if we return for a moment to the women in the poem of Herondas.[25]

The women had brought a thankoffering [26] for the cure of a sick man. They had risen early in the town an hour distant in order to reach the temple in the cypress grove before dawn. The offering was a rooster, a characteristic sacrifice to Asklepios [35]; its symbolic value is expressed in its relation to the sunrise. The rooster is sacrificed at once. The women cry out: "It is day . . . The temple door is open. The curtain is parted!" Up until then the temple had been closed. The women had already greeted the god, whose statue stood on an altar outside the temple, with the words: "Lord Paieon!" an invocation of Apollo the healer—but his appearance, his epiphany, occurred only when the rooster was sacrificed, when the temple door opened, and the sun rose. The door of the little temple which the women visited (the oldest of the compound) opened to the east; the great altar, which remained the center of the cult even after the sanctuary had been extended, also faced eastward. The temple of Asklepios in the sanctuary at Epidauros

35. *Statue of Asklepios. The god is accompanied by a child who carries a cock and a sacrificial knife. This work stands in the Roman Forum, in front of the House of the Vestal Virgins, close to the fountain of Juturna. ca.* A.D. *150*

had the same orientation, while the great peristyle was turned somewhat southeastward, toward the Kynortion, the Mountain of the Rising Dog. At a later date the morning song of Asklepios was incised on a marble tablet in the Asklepieion at Athens.[27] "Awaken, Paieon Asklepios," it begins, and the closing words are: "Awaken and hear thy hymn!" This god's relation to the sunrise, his appearance as a kind of solar epiphany, could scarcely be made clearer. Scholars were long puzzled as to the meaning of Sokrates' strange last words: "Krito, we owe a cock to Asklepios; pay it and do not neglect it." [28] Today we know what he meant. He might just as well have said: "The sun is rising, the light is coming, let us give thanks."

36. *Asklepios. This statue has excited great admiration and was considered a copy of the work by Myron. Our Type* I. *Roman work of the* II *century* A.D.

37/38. *Details of the statue of Asklepios* (36), *Type* I

The rising sun was the great nature symbol of that mysterious divine principle that the Asklepiads of Kos revered in their family cult. The clarity and purity of mind that distinguish the writings of the Koan school of physicians, published under the name of Hippokrates,[29] present no contradiction to this. When the author of the dissertation on the "sacred malady" professes that for him all diseases are human and divine,[30] this does not mean "natural and supernatural," but "natural and for this very reason divine." And these physicians' awareness of the divinity of their art must be understood in the same sense. A later treatise,[31] on "Decorum," shows this same sense of the natural and divine: "Wherefore . . . transplant wisdom into medicine and medicine into wisdom. For a physician who is a lover of wisdom is the equal of a god." The power to help, unless accompanied by the inner clarity of knowledge, or for that matter the knowledge of the philosophers alone without ability to help, would not make a physician godlike.[32] The divine physician, who combines light and helpfulness in his person, is Asklepios, ancestor and prototype of all mortal physicians.

39. *Asklepios. Type* II. *Roman, age of Syracuse. Probably copied from the statue made by Alkamenes ca. 400* B.C. *for the Asklepieion of Athens. Note the omphalos, below, at the left of the god. The omphalos is generally associated with Apollo*

40. *Asklepios. Second example of Type II. Roman work dating ca. A.D. 150. Copy after the same Greek original as 39*

41. *Asklepios. Type* IIa.
Copy after the original
of Type II, *except for the*
beardless head of a young
man. The representation
of Asklepios as a young man
was not rare in antiquity.
This Roman transformation
of an otherwise bearded type
is striking

42.   *Head of the statue of Asklepios (41). Type IIa*

43. *Asklepios. Type* III.
*Classicistic work dating from
ca.* A.D. *130. It is a synthesis
of the writer-physician
and the divine seer. This
statue was probably copied
from an original of the early
*IV *century* B.C.

44. *Detail of 43,*
Type III

There are portraits of Asklepios antedating the Melos head and most
of the Epidaurian likenesses. Some were created in Athens as early as
the fifth century, in the great period of classical art. The heads are both
bearded and unbearded. On the preceding and the present pages the
reader may find a selection of the types that the god assumed for eminent Greek artists [36–44].[33] They are followed by a portrait [45] discovered on Kos and thought to represent Hippokrates.[34]

A certain significance also attaches to the reports of golden wreaths
that were bestowed on physicians at the height of their careers. According to the legend, Hippokrates was crowned with a golden wreath valued
at a thousand gold pieces [35] when the Athenians invited him along

67

45. *Hippokrates. This
statue, found on the
island of Kos, is the work
of an artist of the* IV *century*
B.C. *Discounting the bad
restoration of the tip of the
nose, there is a striking
resemblance to the portrait
of Hippokrates on coins from Kos*

with his son Thessalos, to participate in the Eleusinian Mysteries as an
official guest of honor.[36] There was also a crown on the colossal head of
Asklepios in the grotto in Melos and we shall speak later on of a
wreathed statue of Machaon, son of Asklepios. A golden wreath always
represents rays and symbolizes the sunlike. Such an honor, even if
legendary, bears witness to what in the living religion of Asklepios
constituted the special nature of the Asklepiad, the true physician. For
the medical gift that the Asklepiads held they had inherited from their
solar ancestor is a very special gift: it is neither a religious nor a philo-
sophical knowledge; indeed it cannot be set down as any sort of de-
partmentalized knowledge, but is rather a familiarity, which can

never be acquired, with sickness and the process of recovery. It is a spark of intuitive knowledge about the possibilities of rising from the depths, a spark which by observation, practice, and training can be fanned into a high art and science: into a true art of healing. The religion of the Koan physicians was directed toward this spark and its sun-like efflorescence. In the following pages we shall look into the mythological expressions of this primeval age of medicine.

IV. HERO PHYSICIANS AND
THE PHYSICIAN OF THE GODS
IN HOMER

O U R search for the traces of the religion of Asklepios has led us from Rome to Epidauros and then eastward to the isle of Kos. We shall also have to take a brief trip to Asia Minor for a look at the Asklepieion of Pergamon. But we must not forget the region and the city that formed the center of the Greek world, Attica and Athens, nor the great poetry and legends of Homer or the heroic epics associated with his name. With these the Asklepiads of Kos felt as closely related by their family traditions as with the cult of their divine ancestor. On the one hand we have Homeric poetry and on the other hand cult legends from an Asklepieion or—to mention the more archaic form of the Koan sanctuary—from a sacred grove of Apollo Kyparissios. These two totally different types of narrative disagree on one essential point. For Homer and the epic poets of the Homeric school Asklepios was not a god but a mortal hero; a hero who died and only when dead was venerated like dead royal heroes. In his lifetime he was only an "excellent physician." [1] We shall learn in Attica what the religious veneration of such a medical hero meant; as for the explanation of the contradiction we shall find it in Homer himself.[2]

Asklepios made his solemn entry into Athens in the year 420 B.C.;[3] his sanctuary was built in a spot sheltered from the wind on the southern slope of the Akropolis, not far from springs which are still thought to possess curative qualities. Here he settled with his family, the goddesses Hygieia and Epione [46] and his sons. He sometimes appears at

46.   *Fragment of a votive relief representing Asklepios accompanied by two goddesses. ca. 390* B.C.

47. *Votive relief from Thyrea, in Argolis, showing at the right the whole family of Asklepios. Behind Asklepios, Hygieia, whose silhouette is barely visible; then the god's two sons, Machaon and Podaleirios, and three goddesses, possibly identified as Akeso, Iaso, and Panakeia (cf. 23). ca. 370–360 B.C.*

the head of the whole procession of gods [47]. But in Attica other more-than-human physicians were also revered. In the days of Lucian the satirist (second century A.D.) a monument to the "Foreign Physician" [4] stood not far from the great double gate, the Dipylon; it reminds us of the itinerant Koan physicians who set down their experiences in a book called "Epidemics" (Ἐπιδημίαι), and of the legendary thaumaturges such as Pythagoras and Abaris the Scythian, who were looked upon as embodiments or emissaries of Apollo. But there was also an indigenous form of mythical physician; this was a "hero" in the Homeric manner.[5] An inscription in Athens calls him the *heros iatros*, the "hero physician," adding the epithet "he who is in the city" (ὁ ἐν ἄστει). This specific allusion to the site of the cult is at the same time a reference to an institution represented both in the city itself and in the Attic countryside. We gain an idea of the institution itself from two longer inscriptions both of which refer to the inventory of the objects contained in the sanctuary of the *heros iatros.*[6]

The one inscription, dating from the end of the second century B.C., speaks of a sacrificial cist, a wine pitcher, two goblets, a censer, and a bowl that have fallen into poor condition, and of votive figurines of metal, chiefly limbs, that have been melted down under official super-vision. New ritual utensils have been made from the metal. The other inscription, dating from the year 222/221, lists the melted votive ob-jects and gives the names of persons who have been cured or have es-caped from war and shipwreck—a small shield and a fragment of a ship indicate such rescues. The inscription also notes the new ritual utensil: a large silver wine pitcher. To judge by these two inscriptions, wine played an important role in the ceremonies of sacrifice to the "hero physician"—who in the second inscription is also called a "god." We recall the Dionysian painting in the rotunda at Epidauros (p. 45), and thus we cannot help but wonder what relation there was between the *heros iatros* and Dionysos and his circle.

In Athens this relation between the spheres of Asklepios and Diony-sos is reflected by the proximity of the Asklepieion to the theater of Dio-nysos and in nearby Marathon by the situation of the tomb of the *heros iatros* beside the sanctuary of Dionysos.[7] In other words, we have a chthonic and a Dionysian sanctuary side by side. We even know the name of him who was honored in the tomb cult. He bore the same name as the "*heros iatros* in the city." But before we reveal it, a word on the significance of such names.

Aside from Athens and the village of Marathon there were other places in Attica that had their hero physicians. Among these were Eleusis and Rhamnous. A late tradition [8] records the name of the Eleusinian *heros iatros* as Oresinios. This, it is expressly stated, is the name of a physician who once lived. We may therefore assume that if the cult of his tomb became the cult of a divine physician it was because of the facts of his life. In this case the memory of the healer's activity lent a new, personal trait to the figure of the *heros iatros*, who had been venerated from time immemorial. But originally "heroes" were not recruited from deceased physicians or mortals of other classes; they were the heroes of the legendary past as portrayed first in the Homeric epics and later in Attic tragedy. Even the physicians among them were primarily warriors and leaders of armies. Consequently the name of the *heros iatros* in Athens and Marathon is a hero's name that links its holder with the old warrior heroes. He was called Aristomachos, "the best warrior," a name more typical than individual. Aristomachos was not a hero often celebrated in song, such as Amphiaraos, the seer and divine healer worshiped in nearby Oropos, who gradually came to overshadow him. In Rhamnous too he was called Amphiaraos, or he was taken to be Amphilochos, a son of Amphiaraos.[9]

With all these epic-heroic names we seem to be far removed from the Dionysian circle, but not from the family traditions of the Koan physicians. We now leave Attica, the Athenian excavation sites with their fragrance of camomile, and the heady pine country between Oropos and Eleusis. Pausanias tells us of hymns that were sung in the sanctuary of Asklepios in Pergamon,[10] and these hymns mention a hero, from among the heroes of epic and tragedy, who is related in a

very special way to the secrets of the healer's art. Here we cannot accord
him the detailed mythological study he deserves, but we shall need at
least a passing acquaintance with him if we are to gain an idea of the
manifold relations between these two seemingly so different worlds,
the world of the heroes and that of the Asklepiads.

I am speaking of Telephos, who, having been wounded by Achilles,
was informed by the oracle of Apollo that he who had wounded him
would also make him well.[11] He was the defender of the region in Asia
Minor where the magnificent city of Pergamon later arose and was
wounded by the advancing Greeks who were mistakenly looking for
Troy in this spot. The festive hymns in the Asklepieion of Pergamon
began with his name—not only because he was the most famous hero
of the place but also, no doubt, because his history,[12] known in many
variants, had taken on particular meaning for the descendants of
Asklepios. Telephos, made famous by the strange episode of the
wounded healed by the wounder, was connected with Apollo, the stag,
and the cypress. His foster father was named Korythos,[13] otherwise a
surname for Apollo; Apollo Korythos was indeed a healer god in Messenia.[14] As a child, Telephos had been abandoned and suckled by a doe.
His name meant the "far-shining"; his mother's name was Auge, "the
light." One of his sons was Apollo's favorite, Kyparissos, who killed his
beloved stag by mistake and turned himself into a cypress. All these
traits, mythological variants of the sun's birth, of the daily and yearly
epiphany of the light, preceded by a death of the light at the winter
solstice, were symbols of recovery and the sunlike genius that brings it
about. This is why they had their place in a hymn to Asklepios.

Pausanias also gives us a piece of negative information; he tells us that one son of Telephos was not permitted to be named—let alone sung—in the temple; but this merely proves that the hymn beginning with the name of Telephos concerned the Asklepiads. This son had a name which obviously connected him with the realm of the dead: Eurypylos, "he with the wide gate." The *Little Iliad* [15] tells us that he killed Machaon, a son of Asklepios and one of the hero physicians mentioned in the Iliad. Machaon was the first surgeon, while his brother Podaleirios healed "invisible" ills, including those of the soul.[16] The post-Homeric epic poet Arktinos, our source for this bit of information, gives the brothers Poseidon for father—a strange divergence from the traditions of the Asklepiads who agreed with Homer on this particular point, revering Podaleirios and Machaon as their two great ancestors, the first sons of Asklepios. But we should not be surprised at the divergence, nor at Homer's reticence, which we shall discuss in a moment. For Homeric poetry carefully excludes mythological elements of the kind that we have encountered in the course of our investigations.[17]

When we turn to Machaon, the first surgeon, we shall no longer, as in studying the mythology of the other divine Greek physicians, concern ourselves predominantly with the living and life-giving element that flares up against a darker background, but with the deadly, murderous background itself. Machaon, a *heros iatros* in the original sense of the words, bears as warlike a name as Aristomachos: his name might be rendered as the "slaughterer," from the same root as the Greek word for battle, μάχη.[18] Other healer gods or heroes, who pass as sons of Machaon, bear names more suggestive of war, such as Polemokrates,[19] "ruler of war," and Nikomachos,[20] "victor in battle." Warriors and physicians in one person, they express a unity. Wounding and being wounded

are the dark premises of healing; it is they that make the medical profession possible and indeed a necessity for human existence. For this
existence may—among many other possibilities—be conceived as that
of a wounding and vulnerable being who can also heal, while the animal
is merely wounding and vulnerable. But it is only man's wounds that
can be healed, not man himself. Machaon wounds and heals, but in
essence he is incurable. Eurypylos, the underworld ruler "with the wide
gate," engulfs him forever. The warrior surgeon dies of his wounds.
But in the cult of his tomb he lives on, attaining to the existence of the
Greek gods, wounding and vulnerable, healing and susceptible of being
healed.

In Attica and in other regions of Greece that were not favored with
a primordial medical culture like that of Kos, such hero physicians
degenerated into vulgar thaumaturges. But their original character appears in the rich fabric of mythology and heroic legend. It should not
surprise us that in the ancient traditions that go back to the family tradition of the Asklepiads, to their mythological knowledge of the foundations of their own mode of existence—the physician's existence—relatively little is said about the dark depths. Such knowledge naturally and
immediately implies silence, although the greatest secrets of human
existence always remain in a sense open secrets. Perhaps in these reflec-
tions we are really speaking of a kind of medical secret—the secret
of the autodiagnosis which for the early physicians of Greece assumed
the form of gods and heroes and their destinies. The poets also helped
the Greek physician to such self-knowledge: first the creators of the
mythologems, then Homer with his profound, all-embracing knowledge
of human existence. The Iliad is the great epic of wounding and being

wounded—in a word, of war. And when it comes to the sufferings and hardships of heroes, it is not silent.

Students of Homer have always been struck by the abundance of surgeons in the Iliad. To be sure, the wounded—for example, the companions of Idomeneus in Book XIII (210–14)—must be brought to them, but there are always plenty of them about and their presence is taken for granted. Certain scholars have regarded these passages as late interpolations and wished to restore the poem to its original form by expunging all these nameless surgeons.[21] They failed to see that the passages in question reflect a necessary and natural phase in the development of surgery. For it is self-evident that under archaic conditions the two varieties of experts on wounds—the warrior and the battle surgeon—must have been closely related. Podaleirios and Machaon, the two sons of Asklepios who appear on the battlefield of Troy with their own little army, combine the warrior and the good physician in their persons.

But in the Iliad the divine originator of the healer's art, standing behind the two sons of Asklepios, is the half-human, half-divine figure of a very archaic god, Chiron [22] the centaur. Asklepios himself is mentioned only as the father of his two sons. In the catalogue of heroes [23] and in Book IV, where Machaon is called to Menelaos,[24] the poet seems to know nothing of a physician god and to look on Asklepios merely as a mortal physician who became a demigod after his death. In connection with Asklepios, Homer speaks of no father, but only of Chiron, the fatherly friend and teacher who had taught Asklepios the use of medicinal herbs. His connection with Chiron does not even distinguish him from other demigod heroes. Achilles himself was a pupil of Chiron and had even passed on the lore acquired from him—his knowledge, for example, of the medicinal herb chironion [25]—to his friend Patroklos. But such allusions to the wise and righteous centaur seem like an effort on the poet's part to conceal what he knew of the god of physicians. It is only from late myths that we learn that Chiron too was wounded—an immortal afflicted with an incurable wound. Asklepios suffered a similar fate: Homer, who observes strict principles of selection, evades Asklepios—for what reasons we shall soon see.

Book V of the Iliad relates the wounds of the gods. Here and in Book XI peaks of action are marked by significant wounds. When the Greeks attain to the height of their power, Diomedes wounds even the gods in the enemy ranks: Book V might almost be called the song of the wounded gods. First Aphrodite receives a painful wound in the hand. And even though her divine suffering dissolves as it were in the smile of Zeus the father,[26] Dione, mother of the wounded goddess, bares deeper mythological wounds in her words of consolation. If we wish to explore this dark aspect of the Greek gods and their world, we must read at least a part of her revelations.[27]

"Endure, my Child, and face your troubles gallantly," says Dione and proceeds to enumerate the sufferings inflicted on gods by violent men. First she speaks of Ares, chained by the giant sons of Aloeus; he made the best of it: "Hera suffered too, when the powerful Herakles, Amphitryon's son, struck her with a three-barbed arrow in the right breast—she had to bear incurable pain." [28] In the cyclic existence of Hera,[29] this wound recurs alternately with its cures. The gods' wounds bring home to us the higher significance of the wound in the Greek view of the world—a significance not confined to the wounded individual.

Dione goes on to speak of a wounded god, Hades, god of the underworld, or Aides as Homer calls him:

"And the monstrous Hades himself was wounded by an arrow, and had to bear it like the rest, when that same man, the son of aegis-bearing Zeus, shot him at the Gate of Hell among the dead, and left him to his anguish. Sick at heart and in excruciating pain, Hades found his way to high Olympos and the Palace of Zeus. The arrow had driven into his shoulder muscles and was draining his strength. However, Paieon the Healer spread soothing ointments on the wound and cured him; for after all he was not made of mortal stuff." [30]

Again the wound is inflicted by the arrow of Herakles. In Homer the realm of the king of the underworld is called Pylos, the "gate among the dead." Hades who has received his wound down below, "at the gate," goes up to Olympos where he finds a physician—the same who heals another wounded god in Book V of the Iliad. This second wounded god is the greatest of wounders, Ares, god of war. Diomedes, aided by Pallas Athene, wounds him "with a spear of flashing bronze." Screaming like ten thousand warriors, Ares flies up to Olympos and is healed by Paieon just as Hades had been and for the same reason: as a god, he must not die.[31]

Who is this divine physician on Olympos who guarantees the immortality of the gods by healing their wounds? Is he simply the medical function, personified and raised up to the heavens? In any case he is not the function of earthly physicians. This function in Homer goes back to Chiron the centaur, who is involved in the un-Olympian world of life and death and remains on earth. Homer draws an inviolable dividing line between the spheres of mortality and immortality. For him even the best of physicians, even an Asklepios or the more godlike Chiron, remains in every respect confined to the realm of mortality. Paieon stands over the physicians. He is a higher source of cure than Chiron or Asklepios. In the Odyssey the Egyptians, those dwellers in an almost mythological country, versed in medicine, are descended from him. One version of the Odyssey connects Paieon with Apollo as though the latter were the true source of the healer's art.[32] But this version did not prevail. Homer and the epic tradition clung to the figure of Apollo the archer with all his dangerous attributes. In this tradition Paieon, distinct from Apollo, was the god of healing, whose light overshadowed that of Asklepios.

As we know from other contexts, the Homeric theology drew a strict dividing line between the Olympian and the non-Olympian, eternal brightness and deadly darkness. Nevertheless both custom and religious doctrine decreed that in all Apollonian sanctuaries the ritual hymn known as the paean after Paieon should be sung in praise of Apollo. This discloses a profound bond between Apollo and the paean. Even in the Iliad the Greeks sing the paean to Apollo to celebrate his forgiveness and the end of the plague that he had sent. The paean does not ward off or dispel the plague; essentially its character is positive, it was a celebration of something salutary. At Delphi the paean was sung from spring to late fall; it was discontinued only in the winter months.[33] But a typical line of the hymn, recurring like a refrain, expresses the wish: "May Paean never leave us"[34]—never let him cease or be absent. Who or what is this Paean?

Surely not the hymn known by that name, that must never cease or be absent. No, the name referred to a positive principle which Homer had placed on Olympos as an eternal god, healer of the wounds of the immortals, so assigning to Paieon a place where there is no ending. And most particularly no ending of what constitutes the essence of the god Paieon. Olympos was the place of eternal light. Not of a purely celestial light, an abstract light so to speak, but of a sunny, warm light, for the gods love the sun even more than we human beings. But Helios, the sun that shines for us mortals, goes down. He loses his strength in winter, and sometimes our father Helios is even eclipsed. "Beam of the sun, what wilt thou be devising?" begins the hymn that Pindar [35] wrote for his compatriots during an eclipse. He sings not to ward off the darkness but to hold fast the light. And what he seeks to hold fast is eternal on Olympos. We should call it the pure healing power of the sun. For the Greeks Apollo was this power [36]—but never exclusively. He also carried with him the bow that wounds and kills. Outside the domain of Homer's theology nothing was more natural than to invoke the helpful Asklepios as Paean and sing the paean to him. But Homer refuses to be corrupted by ephemeral, earthly cures. He well knows that a "healer" like Paieon is present only for the wounds of the gods, while the most that men can hope for is a vulnerable hero physician.

Book XI of the Iliad relates another climax characterized by the infliction of wounds. In it not gods but men are wounded, among them Machaon the physician. And this is the height of calamity. Nearly all the great heroes of the Greeks have already been wounded: Agamemnon, Diomedes, Odysseus. And then a three-barbed arrow strikes Machaon himself in the right shoulder. The venerable Nestor is bidden to convey him quickly from the field of battle to the ships. "A surgeon," said Idomeneus, "who can cut out an arrow and heal the wound with his

48. *Achilles dressing the wounds of Patroklos. Vase painting by Sosias. ca.* 500 B.C.

ointments is worth a regiment." [37] Achilles sees Nestor driving by with the wounded physician, and he knows that his own day has come: the Greeks have been deeply humiliated by Zeus. The physician himself needs a physician. We hear these significant words from the mouth of another hero, whose wound concludes this significant series of wounds. [38] His name is Eurypylos and his wound is bandaged by Patroklos.

We have already heard where Patroklos derived his knowledge of medicine. [39] An eminent Greek painter of the fifth century B.C. adorned a vase [48] with a scene showing Achilles dressing the wound of his friend Patroklos. The patient himself helps the surgeon to bandage the wound inflicted by an arrow that has already been drawn out and is lying by his side. Patroklos bears an archer's quiver. In the Iliad Patroklos fights not with bow and arrow but with a spear. Not even Eurypylos, whose wound is dressed by Patroklos, is an archer according to the Iliad. The most the artist could have derived from Homer is the general inspiration for his portrayal of the wounded wounder, the hero in need of healing, who helps Achilles with his adroit fingers. Thus it has been thought, not without reason, [40] that Sosias the vase painter

followed not the Iliad but the *Kypria*, an epic relating the events leading up to the wrath of Achilles. One of these events was the landing of
the Greeks in the wrong spot in Asia Minor, where Telephos engaged
them in battle. Wounded by Achilles, Telephos was instructed by Apollo
to seek the help of Achilles. And he was indeed healed by Achilles—in
the best-known version, with the help of the very lance that had smitten
him. Patroklos had fought bravely in this battle,[41] and it was here no
doubt that he received the wound dressed by Achilles on Sosias' vase—a
blow dealt by Telephos, who himself had received a famous wound. It
was his son, called Eurypylos like the hero in the Iliad, and bearing this
underworld name by good right, who was later to slay Machaon the
surgeon. The fine vase painting would then be a monument to the
wounding of Patroklos by Telephos.

According to the poems and legends that tell us of Eurypylos, son of
Telephos, it was Machaon, among the sons of Asklepios, who in a manner of speaking succeeded his father in his darker aspect, his connection
with death. He is the earthly counterpart to the heavenly Paieon. The
physician of the gods on Olympos is purely a healer; he has nothing to
do with killing. But the best physician on earth is a hero who wounds,
heals, and is fatally smitten. Machaon had a hero's tomb in the Mes-
senian city of Gerenia,[42] and here a cult was celebrated. Nestor, who
carries him from the battlefield in the Iliad, was ruler of Pylos—the gate,
as it were, of the underworld; he bore the name of Gerenios after that
city. The scholars who suspected that an archaic, pre-Homeric god of
the underworld was concealed behind this Homeric sage were right. In
his original character he is probably identical with the Eurypylos at
whose hands Machaon met his death.

49. *Head of Asklepios.
Type* II. *The almost
turbanlike wreath is
more conspicuous here
than in other examples.
Early* II *century* A.D.

And yet this sanctuary in Gerenia was no abode of death; in it there
was a wreathed statue of Machaon,[43] perhaps the prototype of the
strange headdress of certain statues of Asklepios [49–51]. A *heros
iatros,* such as Machaon became after his death, died—and did not die.
The sanctuary had a special name, the same as the great island of the
sun: it was called Rhodos, a name suggesting the rose, flower of the
sun and with it the sunlike effulgence that we encounter in the cult and
myth of Asklepios and his sacred places. In the light of this tomb and
sanctuary, the situation in Marathon of the tomb of Aristomachos beside a temple of Dionysos no longer seems so surprising. A number of
motifs in the legends of Telephos and Eurypylos point to the Dionysian

50/51. *Head of a youth. The wreath identifies him almost with certainty as Asklepios. This identification is further supported by the facial expression, halfway between Apollo and the underworld god Eubouleus (Amelung). ca.* A.D. *150*

sphere. The Dionysian gift of a vine with golden leaves and silver grapes lured Eurypylos to Troy, there to slay Machaon.[44] And Achilles was able to wound Telephos only because Dionysos had caused a vine to spring up in the middle of the battlefield and had made Telephos become entangled in it.[45] The darkness surrounding these divine wounded, wounders, and surgeons is strangely mingled with the Dionysian element which in its own way suggests not death but the sunny warmth that is concealed within the darkness of the grape and the vine.

V. THE ORIGINS IN THESSALY

IN THE Iliad Machaon and Podaleirios, sons of Asklepios, are at the head of warriors from Thessaly, the region in northern Greece where the Hellenic tribes first came into contact with the pre-Hellenic world of the Mediterranean basin.[1] Of the three Thessalian cities mentioned by Homer,[2] Trikka is the most important. In Herondas's poem the women invoke Asklepios as Paieon, the Olympian physician of the gods, and as the lord of Trikka.[3] For them Kos comes only second among the sites favored by the god. In the opening verses of his paean to Apollo and Asklepios, Isyllos of Epidauros also mentions Trikka; there too, he assures us, the devotees make sacrifices to Apollo Maleatas before descending into the innermost chamber of the Asklepieion.[4] According to Strabo the geographer, the Asklepieion at Trikka was the oldest in Greece, honored by the god's presence more than any other. On the strength of his mythological sources Strabo tells us that Asklepios was born here on the banks of the river Lethaios.[5] If Epidauros was in a sense the Rome of the religion of Asklepios, whence it spread through the ancient world, Trikka may be called its Bethlehem and Thessaly its Palestine, while Kos constitutes a sort of patriarchate, tracing its origin directly back to Trikka. It seems likely that the splendor of Epidauros, the magnificence of its sanctuary, exerted an influence on the original Thessalian sanctuary as it did upon Kos. However, the excavations by the Lethaios have been neither as extensive nor as fruitful as those of Epidauros or Kos.[6] The once Byzantine-Christian, then Turkish, and now once more Greek city of Trikkala stands on the site of the sanctuary, the ruins of which were used as building materials. The presence of four churches, including the city's mother church, in the relatively small space between the akropolis and the spring of Gurna close by the river, bears witness to the immemorial sanctity of this ground.

Although of typical Greek construction, the vestiges of walls that have been found under a late Roman mosaic floor in the east end of the Mitropolis, or "mother church," tell us nothing. We learn more from the objects found at an earlier date in this quarter of the city and from their situation on the southeastern slope of the mountain where a medieval fortress now occupies the site of the ancient akropolis. These objects are characteristic votive statuettes: Telesphoros, the little hooded nocturnal god [52/53], a rooster, herald of the new day, and an infant in swaddling clothes. We are tempted at first to interpret the baby as a votive offering to the god for the cure of a child, particularly if we bear in mind that in Greece to this day small children are made to pass the night in a kind of "temple sleep" at the feet of a wonder-working Mother of God. It is not easy to forget their yellow little faces, once one has seen them asleep in the candlelight on the dais before the icon. But in an Asklepieion, particularly at Trikka, the votive oblation of a swaddled child may have borne a direct relation to the god himself.

The mythological sources concerning the birth of Asklepios tell us more than the archaeological discoveries, and clearly indicate the perspective in which we should view the sanctuary site and indeed the whole region of Thessaly. The river which forms a semicircle enclosing the birthplace of the god on the west, south, and partially on the east bears the name of the underground river of oblivion and security, "Lethe": a distinct allusion to the mythological meaning of the site. Literally Lethe means hiddenness, seclusion. The Lethaios, the "river belonging to Lethe," divides the birthplace of Asklepios as a place

52. *Asklepios and Telesphoros.
Copy after Type* II. *The head of
Telesphoros is not authentic. Early* II
century A.D.

53. *Telesphoros in his
usual form.* II *century* A.D.

"beyond" from the rest of Thessaly, whose great plain, surrounded by high mountains, unrolls before the akropolis of Trikka. But to east-ward—and it was in this direction that the newborn god looked—lay not only the land of the rising sun, the image of his own birth, but the mythologically so significant scene of his begetting.

For the inhabitants of Trikka the sun rose over a chain of mountains which enclosed the lesser Thessalian plain and the lake of Boibeis, cut-ting them off from the world. By this lake, invisible and otherworldly for the dweller in Trikka, overshadowed by the west and north walls of mighty Pelion, occurred the ineffable events preceding the birth of As-klepios and perhaps, as ancients legends (which the literature, for rea-sons of religious awe, mentions but seldom and then with reticence) would lead us to believe, his birth itself. We know the Epidaurian ver-sion from the Paean of Isyllos, which makes it perfectly clear that the name of Asklepios' mother must not be uttered. The two poetic versions of the Thessalian nativity, that of Hesiod which has come down to us only in fragments and that contained in Pindar's third Pythian Ode, translate the most ancient mythology into the epic language of a later day. But there are other traditions, closely bound up with this part of Thessaly, which disclose elements far older than Homer, Hesiod, and the heroic legends.

Translated literally, Lake Boibeis signifies the lake of Boibe. For the city of Boibe located on its shores bears, in dialect form, the name of the goddess known elsewhere in Greece as Phoibe.[7] Thus Phoibe ruled over the waters of the swampy corner beneath the northern and western slopes of Pelion. If we ask a mythologist what the goddess Phoibe meant to the Greeks, he can offer only two indications. In Hesiod's Theogony, regarded as authoritative by the classical Greek religion, the original founder of the Apollonian line was the Titan Koios; his grandson was Apollo, surnamed Phoibos. On the female side first place was occupied by Phoibe the Titaness, wife of Koios; she is the ancestress, and some of the women among the Asklepiads of Kos bore her name. We have a record of a Claudia Phoibe living in the days of the Emperor Claudius.[8] Late as it is, this use of the name must be taken in the same way as the use of such men's names as Nebros or Drako: in both cases the person so named was supposed to reincarnate the mythical ancestor. The second indication is provided by the Roman poets who referred to the moon by its Greek name of Phoibe.[9]

Here we can relate only the barest essentials about this primordial ancestress of the Asklepiads, Phoibe the moon goddess. She is known, above all, for the primordial love story believed to have taken place at the beginning of time by the shores of Lake Boibeis: [10] the union of the primeval goddess, the first woman in the world, with a god representing virility, whom the mythographers, because of his distinctly phallic shape, also called Hermes—the original Herma, as it were, the pristine phallic idol.[11] Other names or surnames were given the goddess, but only names of divinities equated or identified with the moon in antiquity, such as Persephone, goddess of the underworld, or Artemis, the Diana of the Romans. The goddess of Lake Boibeis was also called Brimo like the great goddess of the nearby Thessalian city of Pherai, the northern Greek form of the mystery goddess Persephone, who has so many names because the real one was not allowed to be uttered: she is "the goddess not to be named." In the Mysteries of Eleusis, when the birth of the divine child was celebrated, the priest proclaimed the event with the words: "The queen has given birth to a sacred child; Brimo has borne Brimos." And our witness adds that this meant: "The strong woman has given birth to a strong youth." [12] For "Brimo" and "Brimos" are not common Greek words, but belong to the language of Thessaly, just as here Boibe takes the place of the usual Greek form Phoibe.

The name of the pristine lover on Lake Boibeis is also translated in the classical Greek and Latin sources. In Latin he is called Valens, "The Strong," in Greek Ischys, a word differing only in accent from the common Greek term for "strength." [13] This god representing pristine virility, Hermes, or "The Strong," loved the divine primordial woman, the moon goddess Phoibe or Brimo, "The Strong," and begot the child invoked in Eleusis as Brimos, "The Strong." In Thessaly this child was said to be Koronis's son, Asklepios, who was worshiped at Trikka. For this is the way of the true mythological tales that are not literary inventions. They vary the same theme, employing different names and figures: in this case the theme of the birth of a divine child who—first dark, then bursting into light—springs from the union of the moon goddess with a strong god who dwells in the darkness.

Some of the different names that were given to the goddess refer to the different phases of the moon. In mythology these phases appear side by side as sister figures. There are usually three of them, and their names signify: the waxing moon rising from the darkness; the moon between the two "half moons"; and finally the phase in which it again takes the form of a sickle and vanishes.[14] Thus it is understandable that in Messenia, whither the myth of Asklepios' birth came from Thessaly, the mother should have been called Arsinoë, one of her two sisters Hilaeira, "The Gracious," an epithet of the mild full moon,[15] and the other Phoibe. The first part of the name Arsi-noë suggests the rising from the darkness and so indicates the moment when Asklepios was begotten: a time of darkness when the new moon had just appeared. And this also explains why the mother of Asklepios, according to Isyllos, may be called Aigla, "The Luminous," and yet in her role of Apollo's beloved is known as the "Crow Maiden," as Koronis the dark beauty.

These names have not been reinterpreted on the basis of forced etymologies; their original meaning is quite transparent. The epic poem attributed to Hesiod dealing with the loves of Koronis and Apollo even relates that the crow was originally white and only grew black in consequence of this love story. This fable,[16] which is not confined to Greece, is a mythological expression of the darkening of the moon. The explanation that Apollo had turned the white crow black for bringing him the news of Koronis's infidelity, was a later addition to the original mythological substance of the story, which included the crow beloved. The late version retains the bird—though in a modified role—along with the figure of the girl. The moon goddess is sometimes bright and sometimes dark, and she was dark in her union with her nighttime lover, Asklepios' father. Concerning him, the poetic versions of the myth give us more details. But the epic poets who transformed the mythological material into heroic legend could hardly have the same hero appear now in animal and now in human shape, now in a dark, now in a bright form. If she is to belong to her dark lover, the goddess heroine must be unfaithful to her bright one, who finds his continuation in her luminous child.

The Hesiodic version describes Koronis as a king's daughter who was wading in Lake Boibeis when Apollo saw her and was inflamed with desire for her.[17] Her mother is never named, as though even in the heroic tradition she had been motherless like the primordial maiden of mythology: the first woman.[18] But there is a sinister quality about the male figures surrounding her in the heroic legend. Her father, King Phlegyas,[19] is a son of Ares the war god (though also, to be sure, of the golden goddess Chryse), an incendiary and offender against gods and men, who sets fire to Apollo's temple at Delphi. Her brother is Ixion, another great malefactor: [20] the first murderer and the ravisher of Hera, queen of the gods. He too had to do with fire, for he slew a guest by burning him on a spit, and as punishment for boasting of Hera's love, he was bound to the fiery wheel of the sun. Phlegyas and Ixion are contra-Apollonian figures, embodiments of evil fire, of fire as a force of destruction.

In the Hesiodic version, Phlegyas gave his daughter, already with child by Apollo, in marriage to Ischys, a son of Elatos. The name of Elatos is no less transparent than that of his son, "The Strong," for Elatos means the "pine." To the north of Pelion, on the west slope of Mount Ossa, lay Elateia, city of the pines, with which Elatos and his son may well have been connected. Here was the entrance to the Vale of Tempe, which played a large part in the myth and cult of Apollo. Apollo came hither every eight years in the form of a boy from Delphi, in order to find himself again as it were, and once more, as a ritual formula puts it, to become the "true Phoibos." [21] The close connections between Apollo in his darker aspects and a tree, the cypress, are known to us from his sacred cypress grove on Kos. Cypress and pine meet on Mount Pelion; [22] here it was possible for the symbolic value of the northern tree to pass over to the southern one. In a region con-

54. *The centaur Chiron. Typical archaic representation, with pine and huntsman's quarry. Attic amphora. ca.* 520 B.C.

secrated to Phoibos and Phoibe, Ischys, son of the pine, stands, as Phoibe's lover, close to the dark Apollo. But in the language of heroic legend, the son of King Elatos could appear only as the god's rival and Koronis as the unfaithful bride who, during the wedding ceremony, is slain by Artemis, Apollo's sister. And so she too enters into a connection with the evil, destructive fire; she is placed on the pyre, whence Apollo removes the little Asklepios, born as his mother dies. Apollo entrusts his education to Chiron, the centaur versed in the art of healing, who dwells in a cave on the heights of Pelion.

So much for the Hesiodic version. Pindar[23] stresses the secret love affair between Koronis and Ischys, so providing a still stronger motive for the god's wrath. For him Ischys is a seducer from Arcadia whom the daughter of Phlegyas, hungry for novelty, is powerless to resist. But by making Apollo's rival hail from Arcadia, Pindar reveals something of his original form. In Arcadia we find mythical beings with exact counterparts in Thessaly, their original home, and one of them is Elatos, father of Ischys. He is one of the centaurs, who make their home in Thessaly as well as Arcadia and the high mountains of the Peloponnese.[24] Chiron, the most kindly of the centaurs, has his cave on Pelion and also dwells in the Peloponnesian foothills of Cape Malea. Indeed, there is a strange relationship between Elatos and Chiron. The arrow that Herakles aims at Elatos wounds Chiron mortally in his cave on Malea. According to another tradition, Chiron suffered a similar fate on Pelion.[25] Malea and Pelion are different scenes of the same mythological events. The mighty seducer, Koronis's lover, comes from a primeval centaurian world, whether localized in Thessaly or more southerly regions. Chiron the centaur rules over this realm [54].

In the legend of the birth of Asklepios, the goddess of Lake Boibeis represents a dark sphere, the nocturnal world of birth, where gather the seeds and energies for a more spiritual birth. In the primordial world of mythology the vehicles of such seeds and forces appear as contradictory figures, half or wholly animal, and these figures remain forever bound up with Asklepios [55]. Ischys, "The Strong," who in his original relation to the moon woman was only the male principle, proves also to be Apollo's darker double. As son of Elatos, he belongs to the race of the centaurs. Elatos, "The Pine," is at once a tree creature and a centaur.[26] All in all Chiron, the wounded divine physician who dies in his

55. *Ritual statue of Asklepios at Pergamon. At either side of the god, a young centaur. Work by Phyromachos, represented on the reverse of a medal of Commodus* (A.D. *180–92). Some scholars have found a striking resemblance between the head of this statue and a Roman copy* (57)

stead, seems to be the most contradictory figure in all Greek mythology. Although he is a Greek god, he suffers an incurable wound. Moreover, his nature combines the animal and the Apollonian, for despite his horse's body, mark of the fecund and destructive creatures of nature that centaurs are otherwise known to be, he instructs heroes in medicine and music.[27] Aside from him, only dark, procreative gods are associated with Cape Malea: Poseidon, who also appears in the shape of a horse, and the likewise animal Silenos. But Apollo himself in his role of father, to whom at Trikka and Epidauros sacrifices were offered in advance of those to Asklepios, also bore the surname Maleatas, "of Malea."

Thus we find a strange kinship between Chiron and Apollo. It calls our attention once more to that dark, yet not unspiritual sphere whence, according to Greek mythology, the art of healing arose. Apollo is as close to the Roman Veiovis as he is to Chiron, and the name Veiovis is translated into Greek as the "underworld Zeus." [28] This brings us back to the sphere of Chiron on Mount Pelion.[29] Zeus Akraios, the Zeus of mountain peaks and the sky, was worshiped on the summit of Pelion, but not he alone. The sanctuary whose foundations have been discovered there was divided in two parts. In the southern part stood the temple of Zeus, facing the sun and looking as it were toward the diurnal side of the world. In the northern half lies a cave that can only be the famous Chironion, the cave of Chiron. This division bears witness not only to the nocturnal character of Chiron but also to his high rank in the Thessalian hierarchy of the gods. It is not for nothing that he passed in classical mythology as the son of Kronos, father of the gods and the dryad Philyra, "The Lime Tree." He is a brother of Zeus and shares the world with him.

In Chiron's half of the world lay Lake Boibeis at the foot of Mount Pelion and, beneath his cave, the valley of Pelethronion, famed for its profusion of medicinal herbs.[30] In this valley Asklepios, under Chiron's tutelage, familiarized himself with the plants and their secret powers—and with the snake.[31] Here too grew the plant named "kentaureion" or "chironion," alleged to cure all snake bites and even the poison arrow wound from which Chiron himself suffered.[32] The tragic view, however, was that Chiron's wound was incurable.[33] Thus Chiron's world, with its inexhaustible possibilities of cure, remained a world of eternal sickness. And even aside from this suffering his cave, site of a chthonic subterranean cult, was an entrance to the underworld. The picture to which all these elements, religious and poetic, give rise is unique. The half-human, half-theriomorphic god suffers eternally from his wound; he carries it with him to the underworld as though the primordial science that this mythological physician, precursor of the luminous divine physician, embodied for the men of later times were nothing other than the knowledge of a wound in which the healer forever partakes.

The physicians of the city of Demetrias, to which the sanctuary on Mount Pelion belonged, revered Chiron as the founder of their line[34] just as the Koan physicians revered Asklepios. In another city of Thessaly, however, human sacrifices such as were offered to dangerous chthonic gods were said to have been made to Chiron and to the hero Peleus who also lived in Pelion, though in this form the story is scarcely deserving of credence.[35] Yet Asklepios too is associated with the underworld. According to one legend he was condemned to death for raising the dead and so offending against the inflexible law of Moira; Zeus smote him with his thunderbolt and cast him into the underworld.[36] And at Trikka his epiphany was celebrated as the birth of a divine child by the banks of the underworld river Lethaios. But there was knowledge of a still more mysterious birth that had taken place in the cave of Chironion, namely the birth of the first centaur.[37] The child's father was Ixion, brother of Koronis—still the same mythological

56. *Asklepios on a winged snake as a sun god flaring up out of the darkness. Medal of Alexander Severus* (A.D. 222–35), *from Nikaia, Asia Minor*

sphere, to which Asklepios also belongs. And wherever in Thessaly his birth—the birth of the Apollonian god of healing—was celebrated,[38] Asklepios, precisely in his birth, came into contact with the underworld no less than Chiron.

Pindar saw Chiron as a dead god, and that he was in a twofold sense: first, as a chthonic deity and *heros iatros* who died—and did not die; secondly, in the sense that Greek religion increasingly excluded such contradictory products of the older, more primordial mythology from its pantheon, regarding them merely as characters of heroic legend. Yet the strange contradiction which, for the healers of Thessaly and probably for the Greek physicians of a later day, found its expression in Chiron has remained perhaps a contradiction inherent in the medical art itself. Chiron, the dark god, was able even to restore eyesight,[39] although of course Apollo is regarded as the founder of this branch of medicine.[40] To be at home in the darkness of suffering and there to find germs of light and recovery with which, as though by enchantment, to bring forth Asklepios, the sunlike healer—this is as contradictory as Chiron, and yet it is no less a part of the gift of medicine than the tapping of Paieon's salutary sources of light.

57.   *Head of Asklepios from the Baths of Caracalla. This*
work was formerly regarded as a copy of the head of
Asklepios by Phyromachos at Pergamon—a hypothesis
doubted today. The wreath represented here is not to be
found on the medal of Commodus (55). The head
seems to be a late composite of the characteristic features
of the bearded Asklepios. Late II *century* A.D.

POSTSCRIPT

On Snakes and Mice in the Cults
of Apollo and Asklepios[1]

I SHOULD like here to suggest a hypothesis that may account for the labyrinthine base of the thymele, or tholos, in the sanctuary of Asklepios at Epidauros. In the earlier edition of my *Labyrinth-Studien* I merely remarked that this rotunda deserved a special investigation in conjunction with ancient rotundas in general. Such a monograph had appeared in the *Bibliothèque des Ecoles françaises d'Athènes et de Rome*, fasc. 147 (Paris, 1940). I have in mind the excellent work of Ferdinand Robert, quoted in n. 40 to Chapter II of the present study of Asklepios. Robert's contention that the labyrinth of Epidauros was intended for chthonic blood sacrifices remains, to be sure, indemonstrable, as I remarked in the same note. In the text of Chapter II (p. 45) I also mention a discovery of my own which I believe contributes to an explanation in line with the hypothesis that I am about to advance.

On my last visit to the hieron of Epidauros before the war (1931) I climbed down into the labyrinth to see whether a ritual procession would have been possible there. I found the passage, which makes three circuits with two changes of direction before it reaches the center, too narrow for the purpose, and accordingly I do not believe that sacrifices were made there. At the same time I found among the marble fragments scattered about the labyrinth one representing a tree trunk with a mouse or rat sitting on it. I immediately photographed it and made a sketch. Along with my traveling companions, I examined the piece at length and from all angles. A mistake in observation is inconceivable. The fragment was without artistic value and seemed to be a mere ornament. I took note of where I left it, with the intention of returning soon and examining the other marble fragments as well. Unfortunately I was not able to do so in the ensuing twenty years. The photograph and sketch were destroyed in Budapest during the war. Since the war I have twice visited Epidauros. On these occasions I examined the tholos and searched the museum and storerooms, but without finding the fragment. I can only hope that the reader will accept my testimony.

It seemed reasonable to associate the mouse or rat with Apollo Smintheus. The traditional derivation of the epithet from the Ionic *sminthos,* "mouse," [2] is clear enough. The discovery seemed to confirm the thesis put forward in the present study (p. 29) that Asklepios represented an aspect of Apollo himself. In the text I went no further and merely added the observation that, as we definitely know since the excavation of the Asklepieion of Pergamon, a semisubterranean rotunda was an element in the cult of Asklepios even at a later period.

But what was the purpose of such a rotunda, which—in Epidauros at least—could include a mouse among its ornaments? An animal indispensable to all Asklepieia was the snake. When subsidiaries of the Epidauros sanctuary were established, a sacred snake was solemnly sent to the place in question by carriage or ship. The legend speaks emphatically of *the* snake,[3] although in practice there must have been at least a pair of snakes. To this the monuments of Epidauros and Athens bear witness. The next obvious question is hard to answer at one's writing desk: on what were all these snakes fed? Large snake-breeding establishments are still in existence today. They raise mice as

58.   *A young man catching a mouse*

food for the snakes. Since visiting such an establishment, I regard it as certain that the snakes were raised in the circular structures of the Asklepieia and that the form of these buildings was adapted to their habits. A mouse was an appropriate ornament for such an edifice, for here mice were offered up to the sacred snakes.

In a sense the mice were sacrificial animals, sacrificed to Apollo, who destroyed them and *was therefore called Smintheus*. In his book,[4] Grégoire publishes some remarkable finds which Wilhelm Vollgraff, a Dutch archaeologist, made in the castle of Argos, the site of an archaic cult of Apollo:[5] a number of terra-cotta mice, their eyes sealed with a kind of bandage. These little votive offerings replaced sacrificial animals. Vollgraff himself thought of Apollo Smintheus. For the sake of his hypothesis, Grégoire regards the blind mice as a substitute for moles—and one cannot help wondering why, if moles were intended, the terra-cotta animals are not moles. Actually Vollgraff's finds show us how the mice were delivered to the snakes that were to devour them. One example makes it clear that the mouse could also be fastened by the tail. A hitherto unexplained vase painting [58] [6] shows us a young man catching a mouse—perhaps a ritual sport. On the other hand, we have evidence of snake breeding for the benefit of Apollo himself.[7] It can scarcely be doubted that the snake was a form of Apollo epiphany, although the tradition misleadingly attests it only for Delos.[8]

Like the snake itself, a rotunda with a labyrinthine substructure had chthonic implications. But no more solely chthonic than the snake of Asklepios, which often dwells in trees, and particularly the snake which according to legend climbed a palm tree in the sanctuary of Apollo at Antium, so showing its Apollonian nature. The superstructure was more or less a copy of the heavenly cosmos.[9] The religious meaning of the labyrinth, which leads down into the depths but only in order to combine "below" and "above" into a unity, is revealed also at Epidauros.

NOTES | LIST OF WORKS CITED

ABBREVIATIONS

Used in the notes and in the List of Works Cited. Shortened titles readily identified in the List of Works Cited are not included.

AM   Athenische Mitteilungen (Mitteilungen des kaiserlich deutschen archäologischen Instituts, Athenische Abteilung). Berlin (before 1942, chiefly Athens).

AnnIst   Annali dell'Istituto di correspondenza archeologica. Rome.

ArchRW   Archiv für Religionswissenschaft. Freiburg im Breisgau.

BullICSLon   Bulletin of the Institute of Classical Studies of the University of London. London.

FrStudRKA   Frankfurter Studien zur Religion und Kultur der Antike. Frankfurt am Main.

IG   Inscriptiones graecae. Consilio et auctoritate Academiae litterarum Regiae Borussicae editum. . . . 2nd edn. Berlin, 1873 ff.

JDAI   Jahrbuch des deutschen archäologischen Instituts. Berlin.

JHS   Journal of Hellenic Studies. London.

LCL   Loeb Classical Library. London and Cambridge, Mass. (earlier, New York).

MémAcInscBL   Mémoires de l'Académie des inscriptions et belles-lettres [Institut de France]. Paris.

RE   AUGUST PAULY and GEORG WISSOWA (eds.). Real-Encyclopädie der classischen Altertumswissenschaft. Stuttgart, 1894 ff.

RendLinc   Rendiconti della R. Accademia dei Lincei, Classe di scienza morale, storie e filologia. Rome.

RendPont   Atti della Pontificia Accademia Romana di Archeologia: Rendiconti. Vatican City.

Roscher's *Lexikon*   W. H. ROSCHER (ed.). *Ausführliches Lexikon der griechi-schen und römischen Mythologie.* Leipzig, 1884–1937. 6 vols. in 9 parts, with 2 suppls.

WPZ   *Wiener Prähistorische Zeitschrift.* Vienna.

For full information on the references, including English translations of classical texts, see the List of Works Cited. For abbreviations, see the list on p. 109.

PREFACE

1 To the second edition of *Der göttliche Arzt* (Darmstadt, 1956).

2 Hausmann, p. 18, attacks this thesis.

3 Edelstein, I, 93.

4 *ArchRW*, VII (1904), 6–32.

5 Ventris and Chadwick, "Evidence for Greek Dialect in the Mycenaean Archives," *JHS*, LXXIII (1953), 95.

6 Nilsson, *Geschichte der griechischen Religion*, I, 159.

7 Kerényi, "Miti sul concepimento di Dioniso," *Maia*, IV (1951), 12; etymology according to Kretschmer, "Semele und Dionysos," in *Aus der Anomia*, pp. 18 ff.

8 Kerényi, *Die Herkunft der Dionysosreligion nach dem heutigen Stand der Forschung;* the reading *labyrinthoio potnia* after L. R. Palmer, "Observations on the Linear 'B' Tablets from Mycenae," *BullICSLon*, II (1955), 40.

9 See Kerényi, "Die Schichten der Mythologie und ihre Erforschung," *Universitas*, IX (1954), 637, and "Miti sul concepimento di Dionisio," *Maia*, IV (1951), 1.

10 See Kerényi, "Symbolismus in der antiken Religion," in *Filosofia e Simbolismo;* and Kerényi, *La Religion antique*, pp. 205 f.

11 See Kerényi, *Das Ägäische Fest*, 3rd edn.

12 One of these is quoted in ch. ii, n. 24.

13 See Jung and Kerényi, *Essays on a Science of Mythology;* Kerényi, *Niobe*, Preface, and *Umgang mit Göttlichem*.

14 Otto, *Die Musen* . . . , pp. 72 ff.

15 *Apollon*, 3rd edn., p. 87.

16 Of the little find mentioned on p. 46, I have spoken at greater length in the Appendix to my *Labyrinth-Studien*, which I have added in paraphrase as a postscript to the present volume.

17 *De Télesphore au "moine bourru."*

I. ASKLEPIOS IN ROME

1 Monograph: M. Besnier, *L'île tibérine dans l'antiquité;* chief dates in the island's history during the Middle Ages and later: ibid., pp. 3 ff., and K. Baedeker, *Rome and Central Italy* [1930], p. 302; monuments: L. Homo, *La Rome antique,* p. 336; H. Jordan, "Sugli avanzi dell'antica decorazione dell'Isola Tiberina," *AnnIst,* XXXIX (1867), 389 ff.; new discoveries: M. Marella, "Notizie intorno a 5 statue rinvenute nell'Isola Tiberina," *Notizie degli scavi di antichità,* 1943, pp. 265 ff.

2 Pausanias V 11 11 (tr. Frazer, I, 253). We possess two panegyrics by Aelius Aristides, a great admirer of Asklepios during the second century A.D., celebrating the well and the water of the Asklepieion at Pergamon (orations 39 and 53). All these sources and those to be quoted later concerning Asklepios may be found in the work of E. J. and L. Edelstein, *Asclepius: A Collection and Interpretation of the Testimonies,* I. My presentation of Asklepios, *Der göttliche Arzt* ("The Divine Physician"), had been largely completed when that work appeared, and it did not lead me to make any changes in my text.

3 Hippokrates I 1 (tr. Jones, I, 298 f.).

4 Livy X 47 and Periocha XI (tr. Foster, IV, 540 ff.); Valerius Maximus I 8 2 (ed. Kempf, pp. 44 f.); Anonymous (Aurelius Victor), *De viris illustribus* 22 1–3 (ed. Pichlmayr, pp. 38 f.); Ovid, *Metamorphoses* XV 622–744 (tr. Humphries, pp. 384 ff.); see Ernst Schmidt, *Kultübertragungen,* and Georg Wissowa, *Religion und Kultus der Römer.* Wissowa rightly remarks that Schmidt's critique of the tradition far overshoots the mark.

5 Livy X 47: *Multis rebus laetus annus vix ad solacium unius mali, pestilentiae urentis simul urbem atque agros, suffecit.* "The year had been one of many blessings, which yet were hardly a consolation for one misfortune—a pestilence which scorched both city and countryside."—Tr. Foster, IV, 540 f., modified.

6 Homer, Iliad I 49–52 (tr. Rieu, modified, p. 24).

7 Telephos, wounded by Achilles, receives from the oracle the sentence: ὁ τρώσας καὶ ἰάσεται—Leutsch and Schneidewin, *Paroemiographi,* II, 763, no. 28; Preller and Robert, *Griechische Mythologie,* II, pt. 3, 1139, n. 2. In regard to this motif and examples from Klaros, see O. Weinreich, *Antike Heilungswunder,* pp. 147 ff.

8 See K. Buresch, *Klaros,* pp. 10 f. and 81 f.; Weinreich, op. cit., p. 150.

9 In regard to the snake on the tree trunk in the background, possibly added by the Roman copyist, see Kerényi, "Apollo Epiphanies," in *Spirit and Nature,* pp. 72 f. (where "bears a snake" is a simplification of the translator), and *Niobe,* pp. 181 ff.

10 For this meaning of *religio*, see W. F. Otto, "Religio und Superstitio," *ArchRW*, XIV (1911), 406–22; Kerényi, *Die antike Religion,* 3rd edn., pp. 74 ff.

11 Ovid, *Metamorphoses* XV 628 ff.; tr. Humphries, pp. 384 f.

12 Macrobius, *Saturnalia* I 17 15 (ed. Eyssenhardt, p. 89); Wissowa, p. 294.

13 *Metamorphoses* XV 659 ff.; tr. Humphries, p. 385.

14 *Inscriptiones graecae*, IV ² 1 121–27; German translation and commentary by R. Herzog, *Die Wunderheilungen von Epidauros*. See also O. Weinreich's commentary in Dittenberger's *Sylloge inscriptionum graecarum*, 3rd edn., III, 310 ff., nos. 1168 ff.

15 *Plutus*, lines 400–13 and 633 ff. (tr. Rogers, III, 398 ff., 422 f.).

16 *Metamorphoses* XV 666 ff.; tr. Humphries, p. 386.

17 *Apocalypse*, p. 160.

18 Callimachus, Hymn IV, "To Delos," line 210 (ed. and tr. Mair, pp. 102 f.); Kerényi, "Apollo Epiphanies," in *Spirit and Nature*, p. 57.

19 Aelian, *De natura animalium* XI 3 (ed. Hercher, p. 271); Kerényi, op. cit., p. 69.

20 Jakob Flach, "Ungereimtes Maienlied," *Annabelle*, VII (1944), no. 75. According to Pausanias (II 28 1; Frazer, I, 113), this "fairer" species of snake was found only at Epidauros.

21 *Metamorphoses* XV 729 ff.; tr. Humphries (modified), pp. 387 f.

22 XV 742: *Phoebeius anguis.*

23 J. J. Bachofen, *Beiträge zur Geschichte der Römer* (Gesammelte Werke, I), 104.

24 See Wissowa, p. 308.

25 Livy II 5 2 (tr. Foster, I, 230 f.); Dionysius of Halicarnassus V 13 (tr. Cary, III, 40 ff.); Plutarch, *Publicola* 8 (*Lives*, tr. Perrin, I, 520 f.); see L. Euing, *Die Sage von Tanaquil*, pp. 40 ff.

26 F. Altheim, *A History of Roman Religion*, pp. 207 ff., after A. von Blumenthal, *Hesych-Studien*, p. 38.

27 Altheim, pp. 212 f.

28 On January 1 temples were consecrated to both gods on the Tiber Island; to Aesculapius in 291 B.C., to Vediovis in 194 B.C. The inscription quoted is that of a calendar (Fasti Praenestini): *Corpus inscriptionum latinarum*, I², pt. 1, p. 231; see also C. Koch, *Der römische Juppiter*, pp. 81 f.

29 Servius, *Commentarii in Virgilium* XI 785 (ed. Lion, II, 49); Wissowa, p. 238; Altheim, work cited in n. 26.

30 The essential connection between the two gods is proved not only by the common "birthday" of their temples, the significant January 1, but also by the remarkable fact that by a decree of the Emperor Claudius the sick slaves who

were set out on the island were set free when cured; see Suetonius, *Claudius* xxv 2 (ed. Rolfe, II, 50 f.); Cassius Dio LX 29 (ed. Dindorff, III, 367). The healing god was Aesculapius; the liberator was Vediovis, who was generally associated with the right of asylum and the protection of slaves; see Altheim, p. 262; Koch, *Der römische Juppiter*, p. 78; Kerényi, *Die antike Religion*, 3rd edn., p. 180. The connection between healing and liberation bears witness to a single sacred sphere, shared by the two gods.

31 Livy IV 25 3, 29 7, XL 51 6 (tr. Foster, II, 334 f., 158 f.); Wissowa, p. 294. For the invocations of the Vestal Virgins, see Macrobius, *Saturnalia* I 17 15.

II. EPIDAUROS

1 Pausanias VI 20 2–4 (tr. Frazer, I, 313).

2 The following description of the hieron of Epidauros is based on Pausanias II 27 (tr. Frazer, I, 112), Frazer's commentary in *Pausanias's Description of Greece*, III, 236 ff., and observations of the author, who has visited the sanctuary several times.

3 See P. Wolters, "Darstellungen des Asklepios," *AM*, XVII (1892), 1–15, and the paper, written in the same period, of H. Brunn, "Asklepios und Zeus," *Griechische Götterideale*, pp. 96–110.

4 Wolters, op. cit.

5 Frazer, III, 236 ff., after P. Cavvadias, *Fouilles d'Epidaure.*

6 See Herzog, *Die Wunderheilungen von Epidauros.*

7 *IG* IV² 1 121.

ΘΕΟΣ   ΤΥΧΑ ΑΓΑΘΑ

ΙΑΜΑΤΑ ΤΟΥ ΑΠΟΛΛΩΝΟΣ ΚΑΙ ΤΟΥ ΑΣΚΛΗΠΙΟΥ

8 W. Jaeger stresses the related Hippocratic idea that there is a natural process of cure, which the physician must encourage until nature helps itself or, more accurately, "hastens to help" (βοηθεῖ); see his *Paideia*, III, 28.

9 Herzog, op. cit. But the god who "hastens to help" (βοηθεῖ) is for the Greeks above all Apollo, to whom they give the surname of Boedromios or Boathoos. The former epithet has passed down to posterity as the name of a month.

10 *IG* IV² 1 128; commentary by Ulrich von Wilamowitz-Moellendorff, *Isyllos von Epidauros.* / The song of Isyllos of Epidauros, carved on a stone tablet exhibited in the shrine of Asklepios, is a text which has caused philologists a good

deal of trouble; yet it is fundamental to my studies. The poet who presented this stone would surely not have accepted the inscription from the stone-carver with a mistake in spelling that destroyed its meaning; much less would he have had the tablet set up in this condition. For this reason I regard the text as a reliable basis for my interpretation (p. 28). On the other hand, a mistake in spelling would not have prevented a Greek from arriving at a correct reading, nor would it have constituted a flaw in the tablet's beauty that might have justified its rejection.

11 Pausanias II 26 3–5 (ed. Frazer, I, 110 f.).

12 *IG IV*² 1 128, 43–45. / For the reasons given in n. 10, I now believe that this passage, the two lines in which Wilamowitz (*Isyllos*, p. 18) noted the "stammering" of Isyllos, should be read—with E. Kalinka (in Diehl, *Anthologia lyrica*, 2nd edn., II, sec. 6, p. 116) and Hiller von Gärtringen ("Ein Schreibfehler im Paian des Isyllos von Epidauros," *AM*, LVII [1942], 230 f.)—as follows:

ἐκ δὲ Φλεγύα γένετο, Αἴγλα δ' ὀνομάσθη.

τόδ' ἐπώνυμον· τὸ κάλλος δὲ Κορωνὶς ἐπεκλήθη.

13 The word κορώνη has the significance of *Corvus cornix* and probably also *Corvus corone*. It can also mean anything crooked or bent. Here it seems more plausible to think of the first meaning, because it is supported (in sense and image) by another proper name, that of the town of Korone; see Pausanias IV 34 5–6 (tr. Frazer, I, 231). We shall see further on that the crow plays a part in the story of Koronis.

14 The literal text: ἐπίκλησιν δέ νιν Αἴγλας ματρὸς ᾿Ασκλαπιὸν ὠνόμαξεν ᾿Απόλλων.

15 See Wilamowitz, *Isyllos*, pp. 91 ff., who has established this meaningful connection between the different surnames. H. Ammann, "ΗΙΚΑΝΟΣ," *Glotta*, XXV (1936), 5 ff., supposes a pre-Hellenic origin. On the name of the island Anaphe, see ἀνάπτω, "to kindle," and ἀφή, "the act of kindling."

16 *IG IV*² 1 198–209, etc., in the sense of "Apollo and Asklepios."

17 After the manner of the golden dog of Zeus, which was stolen by Pandareos or Tantalos. See the variant legends in Preller and Robert, II, pt. 1, 378.

18 Scholiast on Sophokles' *Elektra* 6.

19 Pausanias X 14 7 (tr. Frazer, I, 520); Altheim, p. 261; Kerényi, *Apollon*, 3rd edn., p. 44.

20 Poseidon: Pausanias III 23 2 (tr. Frazer, I, 172); for Chiron, see ch. v, "The Origins in Thessaly"; for Silenos: Pindar in Pausanias III 25 2 (tr. Frazer, I, 175).

21 At Piraeus: *IG* II–III ² 4962.

21a See the testimonies regarding the mythical miracles of Asklepios, his death, and his grave in Edelstein, I, nos. 66–120.

22 Hesychius; see R. Herzog, "Aus dem Asklepieion von Kos," *ArchRW*, X (1907), 225.

23 For details see Kerényi, "Wolf und Ziege am Fest der Lupercalia" in *Mélanges . . . offerts à Jules Marouzeau.*

24 We take the concept of symbolism to be, in this sense, consonant with Goethe, for whom the symbolic is what "coincides entirely with nature" and "what would at once express its meaning," in contrast to the allegorical (*Theory of Colours* ["Zur Farbenlehre"], sec. 916 f., tr. Eastlake, pp. 350 f.). See Kerényi, *Die antike Religion*, 3rd edn., p. 91, and *Griechische Miniaturen*, pp. 27 ff.

25 *IG* IV² 1 122 XXVI (similar to 121 XX). / In regard to *incubatio*, cf. Edelstein and his copious bibliography in *Asclepius*, II, 145 ff., and C. A. Meier, *Antike Inkubation und moderne Psychotherapie.*

26 *IG* IV² 1 121 XVII.

27 Ibid. 123 XLIV (after Herzog, *Die Wunderheilungen*).

28 Ibid. 123, li. 134–37.

29 Ibid. 417, 438, 424–25. In the late period the consultation of oracles also took on features characteristic of the mysteries; see S. Eitrem, *Orakel und Mysterien am Ausgang der Antike*, pp. 66 ff.

30 *Plutus*, lines 639 f.:

ἀναβοάσομαι τὸν εὔπαιδα καὶ
μέγα βροτοῖσι φέγγος Ἀσκληπιόν.

Concerning the epithet εὔπαις ("the beautiful child"), see the synonymous καλλίπαις as epithet for two mystery deities, Kabeiros (Hippolytus, *Refutatio* V 6; tr. Legge, II, 118 ff.) and Persephone (Euripides, *Orestes* 964; tr. Way, II, 210 f.); see also Kerényi, *Der grosse Daimon des Symposion*, p. 30. For φέγγος, the "light" in the sense employed in the mysteries, see Aristophanes, *Frogs* 455 f.:

μόνοις γὰρ ἡμῖν ἥλιος
καὶ φέγγος ἱλαρόν ἐστιν,
ὅσοι μεμυήμεθα . . .

("For the sun bestows such luminous rapture only upon us, the initiate.")

31 Hippolytus, *Refutatio* V 8 (tr. Legge, II, 131 ff.); Kerényi in Jung and Kerényi, *Essays on a Science of Mythology*, pp. 191 f.

32 ἄρρητος κούρα: Euripides, *Helen*, line 1307 (tr. Way, I, 580 f.) and fr. 63 in Nauck, *Tragicorum graecorum fragmenta*; Karkinos in Diodorus Siculus V 5 1 (tr. Oldfather, III, 108 f.); Kerényi in Jung and Kerényi, *Essays*, p. 160.

33 The references in M. P. Nilsson, *Geschichte der griechischen Religion*, I, 620 ff.; Kerényi in Jung and Kerényi, *Essays*, pp. 186 f. The word *Mysteria* signifies in general the festival of veiling; Kerényi, *Die Geburt der Helena*, pp. 51 ff.

34 Jung and Kerényi, *Essays*, pp. 153 ff. and 236 ff.

35 *IG* IV ² 1 122 XLII.

36 Pausanias II 10 3 (tr. Frazer, I, 85 f.).

37 *IG* IV ² 1 122 XXXI.

38 Pausanias II 27 3 (tr. Frazer, I, 112). Aristophanes, *Plutus*, lines 644 f. (tr. Rogers, III, 422 f.), provides a parallel and probably an explanation: the woman who hears the cry mentioned on p. 39 and in n. 30 must quickly drink some wine.

39 Cavvadias, "Ἔκθεσις περὶ τῶν . . . ἀνασκαφῶν ἐν ἔτει 1882," Πρακτικὰ, 1882, p. 81.

40 F. Noack, "Der Kernbau der Tholos von Epidauros," *JDAI*, XLII (1927), 75, regards the inner structure as an ancient sanctuary around which the thymele was later built. A highly rewarding treatment, comprising all the religious rotundas of Greece, is provided by F. Robert, *Thymélè*. However, Robert's theory that the labyrinth was intended for chthonic blood sacrifices cannot be substantiated. Even if this had actually been proved, we should have to ask whether this purpose alone—the offering of blood sacrifices to the gods of the underworld—would account for the labyrinthine form of the building. In regard to the meaning of the labyrinth motif in general (the journey through death and back to life), see Kerényi, *Labyrinth-Studien*.

41 For a discussion of the tholos and this sculpture, see the Postscript on p. 102.

42 See W. F. Otto, *The Homeric Gods*, tr. Hadas, pp. 74 f.

III. THE SONS OF ASKLEPIOS ON KOS

1 See P. Schazmann, *Asklepieion*, published by the Deutsches Archäologisches Institut as *Kos*, I, edited by R. Herzog; also A. Neppi Modona, *L'Isola di Coo nell'antichità classica*.

2 Vitruvius, *De architectura* I 2 7: *Naturalis autem decor sic erit, si primum omnibus templis saluberrimae regiones aquarumque fontes in locis idonei eligentur, in quibus fana constituantur, deinde maxime Aesculapio, Saluti* [that is, to Asklepios and to Hygieia], *et eorum deorum quorum plurimi medi-*

cinis aegri curari videntur. Cum enim ex pestilenti in salubrem locum aegra corpora translata fuerint et e fontibus salubribus aquarum usus subministrabuntur, celerius convalescent. ("First, if for all temples there shall be chosen the most healthy sites with suitable springs in those places in which shrines are to be set up; secondly and especially for Aesculapius and Salus; and generally for those gods by whose medical power sick persons are manifestly healed. For when sick persons are moved from a pestilent to a healthy place and the water supply is from wholesome fountains, they will more quickly recover."—Tr. Granger, I, 31). Plutarch, *Quaestiones romanae* 94 (in *Moralia*, ed. and tr. Babbitt, IV, 140 f.), shows that the elevated position was also the general rule.

3 For reference to an English translation, see n. 25.

4 See R. Herzog, *Koische Forschungen und Funde*, pp. 202 f.

5 See Herzog, *Koische Forschungen*, p. 204; on Charondas, see Diodorus Siculus XII 12 f. (ed. and tr. Oldfather, IV, 396–97 ff.).

6 Kerényi, *Pythagoras und Orpheus*, 3rd edn., pp. 11 ff.

7 Kerényi, ibid., p. 22 ff. Also J. Schumacher, *Antike Medizin*, I, 66 ff.

8 Wilamowitz, *Isyllos*, p. 101; Herzog, *Koische Forschungen*, p. 172.

9 Herodotus VII 99 (tr. de Selincourt, p. 447).

10 Letter XI, written by an unknown author who was still familiar with conditions in Kos. This letter can be found in the Littré edition of Hippokrates' works, IX, and in Hercher, *Epistolographi graeci*, pp. 292 f.

11 Ἀνάληψις τοῦ ῥάβδου. See Nilsson, *Griechische Feste*, p. 411. A description of Asklepios' staff (*dei medici baculum*) as an unplaned branch of a tree is to be found in Apuleius, *Golden Ass* I 4 (cf. tr. Graves, p. 28): *quod ramulis semi-amputatis nodosum gerit* ("the roughly trimmed club that he carries").

12 For the subject in general, see H. Diels, *Die Scepter der Universität;* for details, see Sorlin Dorigny, "Sceptrum," in Daremberg-Saglio, IV, 1115–19.

13 Sacred to Hades: Pliny, *Natural History* XVI 139 (ed. and tr. Rackham and Jones, IV, 478 f.); see also F. Lajard, "Recherches sur le culte du cyprès pyramidal," *MémAcInscBL*, XX, pt. 2 (1854), 199 ff.; J. H. Dierbach, *Flora mythologica*, p. 50; A. de Gubernatis, *Mythologie des plantes*, II, 118; J. Murr, *Die Pflanzenwelt in der griechischen Mythologie*, p. 124; P. O. Gruppe, *Griechische Mythologie und Religionsgeschichte*, I, 789, n. 1; F. Cumont, *La Stèle du danseur d'Antibes et son décor végétal*, pp. 39 f.

14 Aulus Gellius, *Attic Nights* V xii 11 ff. (ed. and tr. Rolfe, I, 414–17); Wissowa, p. 237.

15 Ovid, *Metamorphoses* X 106 ff. (tr. Humphries, pp. 237 f.). Kyparissos is by no means exclusively associated with the isle of Keos. According to another

tradition, he was a Cretan. See Servius, *Commentarii* III 680 (ed. Lion, I, 242); Gruppe, I, 788, n. 6.

16 See Pausanias X 13 5 (tr. Frazer, I, 518) and the coins of Kaulonia showing Apollo with a stag.

17 Cf. Hercher, *Epistolographi graeci*, no. II, p. 284, and the supposed speech of Thessalos, son of Hippokrates, no. XXVII, pp. 312–18, in which the legend of Nebros's son Chrysos is related.

18 The most obvious analogy is that of the Roman *circus*, where similar races were held; on its original religious significance in connection with the ancient Roman sun cult, see C. Koch, *Gestirnverehrung im alten Italien*, pp. 41 ff.

19 Paton and Hicks, *The Inscriptions of Cos*, no. 387, line 27; Herzog, *Koische Forschungen*, p. 200, n. 2.

20 See M. Wellmann, s.v. "Drakon," in *RE*, V, col. 1663, and for the genealogy, Modona, *L'Isola di Coo*, p. 119 (after Pomtow), with further literature.

21 See R. Herzog, *Heilige Gesetze von Kos*, p. 48.

22 See the inscriptions quoted by Herzog, ibid. According to the Scholion on Aristophanes' *Plutus*, line 701, the wife of Asklepios was Lampetie, daughter of Helios; this perhaps is the oldest reference to a wife of Asklepios. See Edelstein, *Asclepius*, II, 87, n. 43. In regard to Lampetie, daughter of Helios according to Homer, Odyssey XII 132 (tr. Rieu, p. 192), see Kerényi, *Töchter der Sonne*, pp. 65 f., and *The Gods of the Greeks*, p. 193.

23 Pausanias II 11 7 (tr. Frazer, I, 88). He is identical with the Genius Cucullatus, a figure found in many parts of the Roman empire. See R. Egger, "Genius Cucullatus," *WPZ*, XIX (1932), 311 ff.; Kerényi, "Telesphoros: zum Verständis etruskischer, griechischer und keltisch-germanischer Dämongestalten," *Egyetemes Philologiai Közlöny*, LVII (1933), 156 ff. (German); F. M. Heichelheim, "Genii Cucullati," *Archaeologia Aeliana*, ser. 4, XII (1935), 187; and W. Deonna, *De Télesphore au "moine bourru."* Cucullatus appears even in the Christian era under the name of Saint Cucufas; see I. Waldapfel, "Martyr occultus," *Lyka-Emlékkönyv*, 1944, pp. 138 ff. (Hungarian).

24 After Pausanias II 11 (tr. Frazer, I, 88), who also identifies Euamerion with Telesphoros. Sacrifices were offered to Euamerion in the Asklepieion of Titane "as to a god," whereas Alexanor, who was associated with him, was honored with chthonic sacrifices "as to a hero" only after sunset. The bright nature of Telesphoros, concealed beneath his dark dress, is manifested in the epiphany related by Aelius Aristides: the opposite wall gleamed as though reflecting sunlight. See J. Schmidt in Roscher, *Lexikon*, V, col. 310.

25 It was published in 1929 in *Herodes, Cercidas, and the Greek Choliambic*

Poets, with an English translation by A. D. Knox, pp. 114–23, together with *The Characters of Theophrastus.*

26 For the following scene, see R. Wünsch, "Ein Dankopfer an Asklepios," *ArchRW,* VII (1904), 95 ff., and R. Herzog, "Aus dem Asklepieion von Kos," *ArchRW,* X (1907), 201 ff.

27 *IG* II–III² 3 4533; P. Maas, *Epidaurische Hymnen,* p. 151, and F. Kutsch, *Attische Heilgötter und Heilheroen* (see below n. 2, ch. iv, "Hero Physicians and the Physician of the Gods in Homer").

28 Plato, *Phaedo* 118 A (tr. Fowler, pp. 402 f.). Compare the preceding story about the "true" world of the Beyond and its "true light" (109 D 7; pp. 376–77 ff.).

29 See Jaeger, *Paideia,* III, 3 ff., for a characterization in terms of the history of ideas which confirms the conception at which we have arrived on the basis of the history of religion.

30 Περὶ ἱερῆς νόσου ("The Sacred Disease"): ἀλλὰ πάντα θεῖα καὶ ἀνθρώπινα πάντα. ("They are all divine and all human."—Ed. and tr. Jones, II, 182 f.)

31 Περὶ εὐσχημοσύνης ("Decorum"): διὸ δεῖ . . . μετάγειν τὴν σοφίην ἐς τὴν ἰατρικὴν καὶ τὴν ἰατρικὴν ἐς τὴν σοφίην. ἰητρὸς γὰρ φιλόσοφος ἰσόθεος (ed. and tr. Jones, II, 286 f.).

32 Ibid.: πολλὰ γὰρ οὐδὲ συλλογισμοῦ, ἀλλὰ βοηθείης δεῖται τῶν πραγμάτων. ("For many cases need, not reasoning, but practical help."—Ed. and tr. Jones, II, 294 f.). See ch. ii, nn. 8 and 9, and the expression τὰ τοῦ Ἀσκληπιοῦ βοηθήματα in no. II of the collection of pseudo-Hippocratic letters in Hercher, *Epistolographi graeci,* p. 290.

33 Our basis of selection is physiognomic rather than archaeological. Except in regard to Type II, the archaeologists do not agree in their artistic evaluation of the originals. To be sure, the statues that have come down to us are without exception Roman copies. In his *Masterpieces of Greek Sculpture,* I, 204 ff., A. Furtwängler attributes Type I to Myron, the great brass founder of the fifth century. He regarded it as an originally isolated figure to which a Hygieia was added later. The group has been preserved only in a careless copy (Rome, Palazzo Barberini; Furtwängler, fig. 60). In his *Zeus und Hermes,* p. 64, Ludwig Curtius looks upon the same statue as a Roman "pasticcio." Thanks to the work of K. A. Neugebauer, *Asklepios,* the evaluation of Type II as "a type of Asklepios created in the middle of the fifth century by an Attic artist" rests on a more solid basis. Arndt, in Arndt and Amelung, *Einzelaufnahmen,* nos. 219/20, tentatively attributes Type III to Praxiteles, although the figure with the book exemplifies a somewhat later, more likely Hellenistic conception of Asklepios. As a draped statue the "beardless" Asklepios in the Braccio Nuovo, or New

Wing, of the Vatican belongs to Type II, although no explanation is available as to why "a classical type of statue was combined with the incongruous head of a youth, possibly an idealized portrait" (Neugebauer, p. 42).

34 Our fig. 45 coincides with the effigies on Koan coins (in K. Schefold, *Die Bildnisse der antiken Dichter, Redner und Denker,* p. 172, nos. 24–25). The somewhat mutilated bust from Porto in the Ostia Museum (no. 98) does not do so. C. Becatti, "Il Ritratto di Ippocrate," *RendPont,* ser. 3, XXI (1945–46), 123 ff., takes the latter to be Hippokrates. Its physiognomy, however, speaks against Becatti's conjecture. But it might be possible that, at Rome ca. 100 B.C., the head which Becatti found in Ostia was thought to be a portrait of Hippokrates.

35 See the supposed Δόγμα Ἀθηναίων, no. XXV in the collection of pseudo-Hippocratic letters (Hercher, *Epistolographi graeci,* p. 311), and the remarks of Herzog, *Koische Forschungen,* p. 215.

36 See the supposed oration of Thessalos, no. XXVII in the collection of pseudo-Hippocratic letters of Hercher, *Epistolographi graeci,* p. 316, 38.

IV. HERO PHYSICIANS AND THE PHYSICIAN OF THE GODS IN HOMER

1 Homer, Iliad IV 194, XI 518, see XI 835 (tr. Rieu, pp. 82, 211, 219). This last passage shows that the epithet ἀμύμων is applied not only to the deceased but, in general, to the good physician who here bears no particular name.

2 A first version of the following may be found in Kerényi, "Heros Iatros," in *Studien . . . : Festgabe für C. G. Jung,* pp. 33 ff., with a critique of the theoretical section of F. Kutsch, *Attische Heilgötter und Heilheroen,* an otherwise useful compilation of source material.

3 *IG* II–III ² 3 4960.

4 Of the ξένος ἰατρός, see Lucian, *Skythes* 1 f.

5 On the changes in the meaning of this word, see E. Rohde, *Psyche,* tr. Hillis, pp. 115 ff. In regard to the *heros iatros,* in answer to the arguments presented by H. Usener, *Götternamen,* pp. 149–53, see Rohde, pp. 150 f., n. 94.

6 Reproduced in the work of F. Kutsch.

7 Bekker, *Anecdota graeca,* p. 262, line 16.

8 Ibid., p. 263, line 11.

9 The inscriptions are to be found in the work of F. Kutsch, pp. 48–52.

10 Pausanias III 26 10 (tr. Frazer, I, 178).

11 Scc ch. i, n. 7.

12 See Preller and Robert, *Griechische Mythologie*, II, pt. 3, 1138 ff.

13 Apollodorus, *Library* III ix (ed. and tr. Frazer, I, pp. 396 f.); Diodorus Siculus IV 33 (ed. and tr. Oldfather et al., II, 446–47 ff.).

14 In the city of Korone, whose name has been mentioned in ch. ii, n. 13, as signifying "crow." Pausanias IV 34 7 (tr. Frazer, I, 231).

15 Fr. 8 (ed. and tr. Evelyn White, *Hesiod, the Homeric Hymns* . . . , pp. 514 f.); Pausanias III 26 9 (tr. Frazer, I, 178).

16 Scholiast BT Eustathius on Homer's Iliad XI 515.

17 Such as the sumptuous pre-Homeric cult of the dead, for which see Rohde, *Psyche*, pp. 3 ff., and W. F. Otto, *Die Manen*, who agrees with him in this point.

18 This interpretation is supported by the names of two of Machaon's sons, which will be discussed below.

19 Pausanias II 38 6 (tr. Frazer, I, 131).

20 Pausanias IV 3 10, 30 3 (tr. Frazer, I, 183, 225).

21 Wilamowitz, *Isyllos*, pp. 45 f.

22 This is the spelling used on the vase paintings; the form found in the literary texts is Cheiron. See Wilamowitz, "Neue lesbische Lyrik," *Neue Jahrbücher für das klassische Altertum*, XXXIII (1914), 242.

23 Homer, Iliad II 729–33 (tr. Rieu, p. 59).

24 Ibid. IV 192 ff. (tr. Rieu, p. 82).

25 See ibid. XI 830–32 (tr. Rieu, p. 219); for sources in regard to this plant, see F. Stähling, *Das hellenische Thessalien*, p. 43, n. 7, and a treatment from the standpoint of botany by J. Murr, *Die Pflanzenwelt in der griechischen Mythologie*, pp. 223 ff.

26 Kerényi, *Die antike Religion*, 3rd edn., pp. 163 f.

27 See Kerényi, *Prometheus*, pp. 16 f.

28 Homer, Iliad V 392–94 (tr. Rieu, modified, p. 102).

> τλῆ δ' Ἥρη, ὅτε μιν κρατερὸς πάϊς Ἀμφιτρύωνος
> δεξιτερὸν κατὰ μαζὸν ὀϊστῷ τριγλώχινι
> βεβλήκει· τότε καί μιν ἀνήκεστον λάβεν ἄλγος.

29 See Kerényi, *Töchter der Sonne*, pp. 136 ff.

30 Homer, Iliad V 402 ff. (tr. Rieu, pp. 102 f.; spelling modified).

31 Ibid. 901 (tr. Rieu, pp. 115 f.).

32 Homer, Odyssey IV 231 f. According to Aristarchus:

ἰητρὸς δὲ ἕκαστος ἐπεί σφισι δῶκεν Ἀπόλλων
ἰᾶσθαι· ἦ γὰρ Παιήονός εἰσι γενέθλης.

The accepted text is:

ἰητρὸς δὲ ἕκαστος ἐπιστάμενος περὶ πάντων
ἀνθρώπων· ἦ γὰρ Παιήονός εἰσι γενέθλης.

33 Plutarch, *De EI* 389 c (*Moralia*, ed. and tr. Babbitt et al., V, 224 f.).
34 Pindar, Paean II (fr. 36, Bowra; also ed. and tr. Sandys, pp. 518 f.). See, for the general question, A. von Blumenthal, "Paian," in *RE*, XVIII, cols. 2340 ff.
35 Paean IX (fr. 44, Bowra; also ed. and tr. Sandys, pp. 546 f.).
36 Kerényi, "Apollo Epiphanies," in *Spirit and Nature*, pp. 62–65.
37 Homer, Iliad XI 514 (tr. Rieu, p. 211).

ἰητρὸς γὰρ ἀνὴρ πολλῶν ἀντάξιος ἄλλων.

38 Ibid. 833–36 (tr. Rieu, p. 219).
39 See n. 25 above.
40 Preller and Robert, II, pt. 3, 1148.
41 Pindar, Olympian Ode IX 70 ff. (ed. and tr. Sandys, pp. 102 f.).
42 Pausanias III 26 6 (tr. Frazer, I, 177).
43 Pausanias III 26 9: καὶ Ῥόδον μὲν τὸ χωρίον τὸ ἱερὸν ὀνομάζουσιν, ἄγαλμα δὲ τοῦ Μαχάονος χαλκοῦν ἐστὶν ὀρθόν· ἐπίκειται δὲ οἱ τῇ κεφαλῇ στέφανος, ὃν οἱ Μεσσήνιοι κίφος καλοῦσι τῇ ἐπιχωρίῳ φωνῇ. ("They name the sacred place Rhodus, and there is a standing image of Machaon in bronze: on his head is a wreath, which the Messenians in their local dialect call *kiphos*."—Tr. Frazer, I, 178.) What the special feature of this wreath was we do not know. Hence we merely call attention to the numerous statues of Asklepios that bear these strange, apparently characteristic wreaths.
44 Scholiast on the Odyssey XI 520 f.
45 Scholiast on the Iliad A I 59; Apollodorus, *Epitome* III 17 (ed. and tr. Frazer, II, 186 f.); Pindar, Isthmian Ode VIII 54 (ed. and tr. Sandys, pp. 504 f.).

V. THE ORIGINS IN THESSALY

1 For the general question, see P. Philippson, *Thessalische Mythologie*, pp. 9 ff.
2 Iliad II 729–31 (tr. Rieu, p. 59).

3 Herondas IV 1 (tr. Knox, pp. 114 f.); the oldest testimonies from Thessaly and the Peloponnese may be found in the work of Leo Weber, "Asklepios," *Philologus*, n. s. XLI (1932), 389 ff. See also Wilamowitz, *Der Glaube der Hellenen*, II, 223 ff.

4 Wilamowitz, *Isyllos*, p. 11, C 4.

5 *Geography* XIV 1 39 (ed. and tr. Jones, VI, 248 f.).

6 See Ziehen, "Über die Lage des Asklepiosheiligtums von Trikka," *AM*, XVII (1892), pp. 195 ff., and E. Kirsten on "Trikka" in *RE*, ser. 2, VII, cols. 146–49.

7 P. Kretschmer in *Glotta*, XVI (1927), 173.

8 R. Herzog, *Koische Forschungen*, pp. 75 and 191 f.

9 S. Eitrem on "Phoibe," in *RE*, XIX, col. 345, n. 3.

10 Propertius II 2 line 11 (ed. and tr. Butler, p. 68); Kerényi, *Hermes der Seelenführer*, pp. 75 ff.

11 Kerényi, ibid., and in Jung and Kerényi, *Essays*, pp. 71 ff.; concerning "her-who-cannot-be-named," see ch. ii, n. 32, above.

12 Hippolytus, *Refutatio* V 8 (tr. Legge, II, 138): ἰσχυρὸν ἰσχυρά.

13 Ἴσχυς and ἰσχύς. Wilamowitz (*Isyllos*, p. 81, n. 54) believes that the name has nothing to do with ἰσχύς but should be considered as an abbreviation, perhaps of Ischomachos. The Latin translation "Valens" (in Cicero, *De natura deorum* III 56; ed. and tr. Rackham, pp. 340 f.) proves that a different opinion prevailed at a time when there was still a living feeling for the Greek language. But whether Cicero or Wilamowitz is right, it amounts to the same thing. Ischomachos, he "who fights with strength," is still ἰσχυρός—though it is put more heroically.

14 Here one should consider the calendar division of the Greek month, not into four weeks but into three decades. See W. Kubitschek, *Grundriss der antiken Zeitrechnung*, p. 28, and W. H. Roscher, "Enneadische Studien," *Abhandlungen der sächsischen Gesellschaft der Wissenschaften*, XXVI (1907), 1 ff.

15 For confirmation of this conception and further parallels, see Kerényi, *Niobe*.

16 For general orientation, see Peuchert on "Krähe" and "Rabe" in *Handwörterbuch des deutschen Aberglaubens*. For the mythological meaning, see W. Schmidt, *Der Ursprung der Gottesidee*, I, 326, "Sonnenfalke gegen die Mondkrähe," and passim; see also the indexes in each volume of this work.

17 Hesiod, fr. 122 Rzach (ed. and tr. Evelyn White, fr. 88 of "The Catalogues of Women and the Eoiae," pp. 210 f.).

18 Kerényi in Jung and Kerényi, *Essays*, pp. 199 ff.

19 Preller and Robert, II, pt. 1, 26 ff.

20 Ibid., 12 ff.

21 Plutarch, *De defectu oraculorum* 418 A, 421 C, and also *Quaestiones graecae* 12 293 B (in *Moralia*, ed. and tr. Babbitt, V, 394 f., 410 f., IV, 184 f.).

22 F. Stählin, *Das hellenische Thessalien*, p. 43, n. 10.

23 Pythian Ode III 25 ff. (ed. and tr. Sandys, pp. 186 f.).

24 F. Bolte, under "Pholoe," in *RE*, XX, cols. 515 f.

25 For the best compilation of all the variants, see [J.] Escher[-Bürkli], under "Chiron," in *RE*, III, cols. 2302–08; on the subject of relations with Herakles, see col. 2305.

26 On the centaur Elatos, see Apollodorus, *Library* II v 4 (ed. and tr. Frazer, I, 192 f.). The trunk of a pine is the usual attribute of centaurs in ancient art; see Preller and Robert, II, pt. 1, 5. According to Thessalian tradition, Elatos, father of Ischys, is already ranked among the Lapithae; see Preller and Robert, ibid., 8 f. Nevertheless, the original figure is "centauric."

27 Preller and Robert, ibid., 21 ff.

28 Wissowa, *Religion und Kultus der Römer*, p. 237; Koch, *Gestirnverehrung*, pp. 41 ff.

29 Preller and Robert, II, pt. 1, 19; Stählin, pp. 42 f.

30 Preller and Robert, ibid., 20; Stählin, p. 43.

31 Stählin, p. 43.

32 Pliny, *Natural History* XXV 66 (ed. and tr. Rackham and Jones, VII, 184 f.).

33 Dramatized by Aeschylus. See Preller and Robert, I, pt. 1, 101; Kerényi, *Prometheus*, pp. 74 ff.

34 The city of Demetrias was founded not much before 293 B.C. by Demetrios Poliorketes. The Demetrian family of physicians, who, according to Heraklides (fr. 60; Preller and Robert, II, pt. 1, 20), descended from Chiron, must have been an older Thessalian line.

35 Preller and Robert, II, pt. 1, p. 20 and n. 5.

36 Hesiod, fr. 125, Rzach (ed. and tr. Evelyn White, fr. 90, pp. 212 f.).

37 Stählin, p. 43, n. 1.

38 In addition to Trikka, the region to the north of Lake Boibeis was also regarded as the birthplace of Asklepios. The Dotian plain is mentioned in the Homeric hymn to Asklepios (XVI 3; ed. and tr. Evelyn White, pp. 440 f.); there, probably, are the twin hills the Didymoi spoken of by Hesiod (fr. 122 Rzach; ed. and tr. Evelyn White, fr. 88, pp. 210 f.); see Stählin, p. 59. Apollonius Rhodius, *Argonautica* IV 616 (ed. and tr. Seaton, pp. 334 f.), calls Lakereia by name. It might be mentioned that this name, with another ending, is a recurrent epithet of the crow. See λακέρυζα κορώνη in Hesiod (*Works and Days*,

line 747; ed. and tr. Evelyn White, pp. 58 f.), and Aristophanes, *Birds*, line 609 (tr. Rogers, II, pp. 190 f.).

39 He is the healer of the blind Phoinix; Apollodorus, *Library* III xiii 8 (ed. and tr. Frazer, II, 74 f.). See Escher, under "Chiron," in *RE*, III, col. 2306. An eye ointment is mentioned under Chiron's name; Celsus, *De medicina* VI 6 20 (ed. and tr. Spencer, II, 210 f.), after Wellmann in *RE*, II, col. 2311.

40 On Apollo as a god of healing, see Ganszyniec, "Apollon als Heilgott," *Archiv für Geschichte der Medicin*, XV (1923), pp. 33 ff.; see also A. Pazzini, "Il significato degli 'ex voto' ed il concetto della divinità guaritrice," *RendLinc*, ser. 6a, XI (1935), 66 ff. In connection with the Apollo cult of the Julians—actually, the cult of Vediovis—Koch (*Der römische Juppiter*, pp. 80 f.) points out that the god who, though ready to be born, is extracted by force from his mother's womb was Asklepios. According to Servius, *Commentarii* X 316 (ed. Lion, I, 568), all infants whose birth necessitated a Caesarian operation were held sacred to Apollo: *omnes qui secto matris ventre procreantur ideo sunt Apollini consecrati, quia deus est medicinae, per quem lucem sortiuntur.*

POSTSCRIPT

1 Adapted from Kerényi, *Labyrinth-Studien*, 2nd edn., pp. 61–63.
2 Scholiast on the Iliad A I 39.
3 Valerius Maximus I 8 2; Ovid, *Metamorphoses* XV 622–744.
4 *Asklèpios, Apollon Smintheus et Rudra*, p. 109.
5 Sophokles, *Elektra* 6 with Scholiast.
6 Tischbein, *Hamilton Vases*, II 42 ff., pl. 17; Lenormant and de Witte, *Élite des monuments céramographiques*, II, 353 ff., pl. 104; A. B. Cook, *Zeus*, I, 424, fig. 306.
7 Aelian, *De natura animalium* XI 3; Diogenes Laertius V 91; cf. Kerényi, *Niobe*, pp. 172 ff.
8 Bode, *Scriptores rerum mythicarum*, p. 209, lines 23 ff.
9 The basic material on ritual rotundas may be found in A. Brelich, *Vesta* (pp. 41 ff.).

LIST OF WORKS CITED

For abbreviations, see the list on page 109.

AELIAN (CLAUDIUS AELIANUS). *De natura animalium Libri XVII.* Edited by Rudolf Hercher. Leipzig, 1864.

ALTHEIM, FRANZ. *A History of Roman Religion.* Translated by Harold Mattingly. London and New York, 1938.

AMMANN, HERMANN. "ΗΙΚΑΝΟΣ." *Glotta* (Göttingen), XXV (1936).

ANONYMOUS (SEXTUS AURELIUS VICTOR). "De viris illustribus." *Sexti Aurelii Victoris Liber de Caesaribus, . . . et Liber de viris illustribus urbis Romae.* Edited by Franz (Franciscus) Pichlmayr. Leipzig, 1911.

APOLLODORUS. *The Library.* With an English translation by Sir J. G. Frazer. (LCL.) 1921. 2 vols.

APOLLONIUS RHODIUS. *Argonautica.* With an English translation by R. C. Seaton. (LCL.) 1912.

APULEIUS, LUCIUS. *The Transformations of Lucius, otherwise known as The Golden Ass.* Translated by Robert Graves. (Penguin Classics.) Harmondsworth, 1956. (U. S. paperback edn., with different pagination, The Pocket Library, New York, 1956.)

ARISTOPHANES. *Birds.* In: [*Works.*] With an English translation by Benjamin Bickley Rogers. (LCL.) 1924. 3 vols. (In II.)

———. *Frogs.* Ibid. (In II.)

———. *Plutus.* Ibid. (In III.)

ARNDT, PAUL; AMELUNG, WALTHER; and LIPPOLD, GEORG. *Photographische Einzelaufnahmen antiker Skulpturen.* 13 ser., Munich, 1893–1932.

AURELIUS VICTOR, SEXTUS. See above, under ANONYMOUS.

BACHOFEN, JOHANN JACOB. *Beiträge zur Geschichte der Römer.* (Gesammelte Werke, I.) Basel, 1943.

BAEDEKER, KARL. *Rome and Central Italy.* English version. 16th revised edn., Leipzig, 1931.

BECATTI, GIOVANNI. "Il Ritratto di Ippocrate." *RendPont,* ser. 3, XXI (1945–46).

BEKKER, IMMANUEL. *Anecdota graeca.* Berlin, 1814–21. 3 vols.

BESNIER, MAURICE. *L'Ile tibérine dans l'antiquité.* (Bibliothèque des Ecoles françaises d'Athènes et de Rome, fasc. 87.) Paris, 1902.

BLUMENTHAL, ALBRECHT VON. *Hesych-Studien.* Stuttgart, 1930.

———. "Paian." *RE,* XVIII.

BODE, GEORG HENRI (ed.). *Scriptores rerum mythicarum.* . . . Celle, 1834. 2 vols. in 1.

BOLTE, F. "Pholoe." *RE,* XX.

BRELICH, A. *Vesta.* (Albae Vigiliae, N.S. 7.) Zurich, 1949.

BRUNN, HEINRICH VON. "Asklepios und Zeus." *Griechische Götterideale, in ihren Formen erläutert.* Munich, 1893.

BURESCH, KARL. *Klaros: Untersuchungen zum Orakelwesen des späteren Altertums.* Leipzig, 1889.

CALLIMACHUS. In: *Callimachus and Lycophron.* With an English translation by A. W. Mair. (LCL.) 1921.

CALZA, GUIDO. *La Necropoli del porto di Roma nell'Isola Sacra.* (R. Istituto de archeologia e storia dell'arte.) Rome, 1940.

CASSIUS DIO. See DIO CASSIUS COCCEIANUS.

CAVVADIAS [KABBADIAS], PANAGIOTIS. " Ἔκθεσις περὶ τῶν ἐν τῷ Ἱερῷ τῆς Ἐπιδαύρου ἀνασκαφῶν ἐν ἔτει 1882." In: Πρακτικὰ τῆς ἐν Ἀθήναις ἑταιρίας ἀρχαιολογικῆς, 1882 (published 1883).

———. *Fouilles d'Epidaure.* Athens, 1893. (Only I was published.)

CELSUS. *De medicina.* With an English translation by W. G. Spencer. (LCL.) 1935–38. 3 vols. (Especially Bk. VI, in II.)

CICERO. *De natura deorum.* . . . With an English translation by H. Rackham. (LCL.) 1933.

COOK, ARTHUR BERNARD. *Zeus: A Study in Ancient Religion.* Cambridge, 1914–40. 3 vols. in 5. (Especially I.)

Corpus inscriptionum latinarum. Consilio et auctoritate Academiae Litterarum Regiae Borussicae editum, I, pt. 2. Berlin, 1863 ff. 15 vols.

CREUZER, FRIEDRICH. *Symbolik und Mythologie der alten Völker, besonders der Griechen.* Leipzig and Darmstadt, 1836–42. 4 vols.

CUMONT, FRANZ. *La Stèle du danseur d'Antibes et son décor végétal: Etude sur le symbolisme funéraire des plantes.* Paris, 1942.

CURTIUS, LUDWIG. *Zeus und Hermes: Studien zur Geschichte ihres Ideals und seiner Überlieferung.* (Mitteilungen des Deutschen Archäologischen Instituts, Römische Abteilung, Suppl. I.) Munich, 1931.

DEONNA, WALDEMAR. *De Télesphore au "moine bourru": Dieux, génies et démons encapuchonnés.* (Collection Latomus, 21.) Berchem-Brussels, 1955.

DIELS, HERMANN. *Die Scepter der Universität.* (Rede zum Eintritt des Rectorats der Königlichen Universität in Berlin.) Berlin, 1905.

DIERBACH, JOHANN HEINRICH. *Flora mythologica.* Frankfurt am Main, 1833.

DIO CASSIUS COCCEIANUS. *Historia romana.* Edited by L. Dindorff. Leipzig, 1864. 4 vols. (Especially Bk. XL, in III.) (The English translation of Dio Cassius's *Roman History* by Earnest Cary, LCL, 1914–27, 8 vols., does not contain the passage referred to in the text.)

DIODORUS SICULUS. *The Library of History.* With an English translation by C. H. Oldfather and others. (LCL.) 1933–57. 11 vols. (Especially Bk. IV, in II; Bk. V, in III; Bk. XII, in IV.)

DIOGENES LAERTIUS. *Lives of Eminent Philosophers.* With an English translation by R. D. Hicks. (LCL.) 1950. 2 vols. (Especially Bk. V, in I.)

DIONYSIUS OF HALICARNASSUS. *Roman Antiquities.* With an English translation by Earnest Cary. (LCL.) 1937–50. 7 vols. (Especially Bk. V, in III.)

DORIGNY, SORLIN. "Sceptrum." In: CHARLES DAREMBERG and EDMUND SAGLIO (eds.). *Dictionnaire des antiquités grecques et romaines.* Paris, 1873–1919. 5 vols. (In IV.)

EDELSTEIN, EMMA J., and EDELSTEIN, LUDWIG. *Asclepius: A Collection and Interpretation of the Testimonies.* Baltimore, 1945. 2 vols.

EGGER, RUDOLF. "Genius Cucullatus." *WPZ*, XIX (1932).

EITREM, S. *Orakel und Mysterien am Ausgang der Antike.* (Albae Vigiliae, N.S. 5.) Zurich, 1947.

———. "Phoibe." *RE*, XIX.

ESCHER [-BÜRKLI, J.]. "Chiron." *RE*, III.

EUING, LUDWIG. *Die Sage von Tanaquil.* (FrStudRKA, 2.) Frankfurt am Main, 1933.

EURIPIDES. Fragment 63. In: *Tragicorum graecorum fragmenta.* Edited by August Nauck. Leipzig, 1861.

———. *Helen.* In: [*Plays*]. With an English translation by Arthur S. Way. (LCL.) 1912. 4 vols. (In I.)

———. *Orestes.* Ibid. (In II.)

FLACH, JACOB. "Ungereimtes Maienlied." In: *Annabelle* (a magazine; Zurich), VII (1944), no. 75.

FRAZER, SIR JAMES GEORGE. See PAUSANIAS.

FURTWÄNGLER, ADOLF. *Masterpieces of Greek Sculpture.* Edited by Eugénie Sellers. London, 1895. 2 vols. (Especially I.)

GANSZYNIEC, R. "Apollon als Heilgott." *Archiv für Geschichte der Medizin* (Leipzig), XV (1923).

GELLIUS, AULUS. *The Attic Nights.* With an English translation by John C. Rolfe. (LCL.) 1927–28. 3 vols. (Especially Bk. v, in I.)

GOETHE, JOHANN WOLFGANG. *Theory of Colours.* Translated by Charles Lock Eastlake. London, 1840.

GRÉGOIRE, HENRI; GOOSSENS, R.; and MATHIEU, M. *Asklèpios, Apollon Smintheus et Rudra: Etudes sur le dieu à la taupe et le dieu au rat dans la Grèce et dans l'Inde.* (Mémoires de l'Académie royale de Belgique, Classe des lettres et des sciences morales et politiques, XLV.) Brussels, 1949.

GRUPPE, PAULUS OTTO. *Griechische Mythologie und Religionsgeschichte.* (Handbuch der Altertumswissenschaft, V, pt. 2.) 2 vols. (Especially I.)

GUARDUCCI, MARGHERITA. "Due Basi iscritte nel Sepolcreto Ostiense dell'Isola Sacra." *RendPont*, ser. 3, XXI (1945–46; published 1946).

GUBERNATIS, ANGELO DE. *La Mythologie des plantes.* Paris, 1878–82. 2 vols. (Especially II.)

HAMILTON, SIR WILLIAM. For the publication of Hamilton's collection of Greek vases (his second such collection), see TISCHBEIN, WILLIAM (ed.).

Handwörterbuch des deutschen Aberglaubens. Edited by E. Hoffmann-Krayer and Hanns Bächtold-Staubli. Berlin and Leipzig, 1927–38. 9 vols.

HAUSMANN, ULRICH. *Kunst und Heiltum.* Potsdam, 1948.

HEICHELHEIM, FRITZ MORITZ. "Genii Cucullati." *Archaeologia Aeliana* (Newcastle-on-Tyne), ser. 4, XII (1935).

HERCHER, RUDOLF (ed.). *Epistolographi graeci.* Paris, 1873.

HERODES. "Mime IV. Offerings and Sacrifices." In: *Herodes, Cercidas and the Greek Choliambic Poets. . . .* Edited, with an English translation, by A. D. Knox. (LCL.) 1929. (Bound with *The Characters of Theophrastus.*)

HERODOTUS. *The Histories.* Translated by Aubrey de Selincourt. (Penguin Classics.) Harmondsworth, 1955.

HERONDAS. See HERODES.

HERZOG, RUDOLF. "Aus dem Asklepieion von Kos." *ArchRW,* X (1907).

———. *Heilige Gesetze von Kos.* (Aus den Abhandlungen der Preussischen Akademie der Wissenschaften, Philologisch-Historische Klasse, 6.) Berlin, 1928.

———. *Koische Forschungen und Funde.* Leipzig, 1899.

———. *Die Wunderheilungen von Epidauros: Ein Beitrag zur Geschichte der Medizin und der Religion.* (*Philologus,* Suppl. XXII, 3.) Leipzig, 1931.

HESIOD. In: *Hesiod, the Homeric Hymns, and Homerica.* With an English translation by Hugh G. Evelyn-White. (LCL.) 1920.

HESYCHIUS. See BLUMENTHAL, ALBRECHT VON. *Hesych-Studien.*

HILLER VON GÄRTRINGEN, F. "Ein Schreibfehler im Paian des Isyllos von Epidauros." *AM,* LXVII (1942; Berlin, 1951).

HIPPOCRATES. [*Works.*] With an English translation by W. H. S. Jones and E. T. Withington. (LCL.) 1923–31. 4 vols. (Especially I, II.)

———. *Œuvres complètes.* Translated into French by M. P. E. Littré. Paris, 1839–61. 10 vols. (Especially IX.)

HIPPOLYTUS. *Refutatio omnium haeresium* [*Philosophumena,* or *Elenchos*]. In: *Philosophumena: or, The Refutation of All Heresies.* Translated by Francis Legge. London, 1921. 2 vols. (Especially II.)

HOMER. *The Iliad.* Translated by E. V. Rieu. (Penguin Classics.) Harmondsworth, 1957.

———. *The Odyssey.* Translated by E. V. Rieu. (Penguin Classics.) Harmondsworth, 1956.

Homeric Hymns. See HESIOD.

HOMO, LÉON. *La Rome antique: Histoire-guide des monuments de Rome.* Paris,
1921.

Inscriptiones graecae. Consilio et auctoritate Academiae Litterarum Regiae Borussicae editum. Berlin, 1873 ff. 14 vols. (Especially II–III ², IV ².)

JAEGER, WERNER. *Paideia.* Translated by Gilbert Highet. Oxford, 1939–45. 3
vols. (Especially III.)

JORDAN, HEINRICH. "Sugli avanzi dell'antica decorazione dell'Isola Tiberina."
AnnIst, XXXIX (1867).

JUNG, CARL GUSTAV, and KERÉNYI, C. *Essays on a Science of Mythology: The
Myth of the Divine Child and the Mysteries of Eleusis.* Translated by R. F. C.
Hull. (Bollingen Series XXII.) New York, 1950. (London, 1951; titled *In-
troduction to a Science of Mythology.*)

KALINKA, E. In: Ernest Diehl, *Anthologia lyrica.* Leipzig, 1942. 2 vols. (Especially II, sec. 6.)

KERÉNYI, C. [in German publications, KARL]. *Das Ägäische Fest: Die Meergötter-
szene in Goethes Faust I.* 3rd edn., Wiesbaden, 1950.

———. *Die antike Religion.* 3rd edn., Düsseldorf, 1952. (Cf. French edn. with
added contents: *La Religion antique.*)

———. "Apollo Epiphanies." In: *Spirit and Nature,* q.v.

———. *Apollon: Studien über antike Religion und Humanität.* 2nd edn., Amsterdam, 1941. 3rd edn., Düsseldorf, 1953.

———. *Die Geburt der Helena.* (Albae Vigiliae, N.S. 3.) Zurich, 1945.

———. *The Gods of the Greeks.* Translated by Norman Cameron. London and
New York, 1951.

———. *Griechische Miniaturen.* Zurich, 1957.

Kerényi, C. *Der grosse Daimon des Symposion.* (Albae Vigiliae, 13.) Amsterdam, 1942.

――――. *Die Herkunft der Dionysosreligion nach dem heutigen Stand der Forschung.* (Arbeitsgemeinschaft für Forschung des Landes Nordrhein-Westfalen, 58.) Cologne and Opladen, 1956.

――――. *Hermes der Seelenführer: Das Mythologem vom männlichen Lebensursprung.* (Albae Vigiliae, N.S. 1.) Zurich, 1944.

――――. "Heros Iatros." In: *Studien zum Problem des Archetypischen: Festgabe für C. G. Jung.* (Eranos Jahrbuch 12.) Zurich, 1945.

――――. *Labyrinth-Studien: Labyrinthos als Linienreflex einer mythologischen Idee.* (Albae Vigiliae, 15.) Amsterdam, 1941. 2nd edn. (Albae Vigiliae, N.S. 10.), Zurich, 1950.

――――. "Miti sul concepimento di Dioniso." *Maia* (Messina), IV (1951).

――――. *Niobe: Neue Studien über antike Religion und Humanität.* Zurich, 1949.

――――. *Prometheus: Das griechische Mythologem von der menschlichen Existenz.* (Albae Vigiliae, N.S. 4.) Zurich, 1946.

――――. *Pythagoras und Orpheus: Präludien zu einer zukünftigen Geschichte der Orphik und des Pythagoreismus.* (Albae Vigiliae, 2.) 2nd edn., Amsterdam, 1940. 3rd edn. (Albae Vigiliae, N.S. 9.), Zurich, 1950.

――――. *La Religion antique.* Geneva, 1957. (Cf. *Die antike Religion.*)

――――. "Die Schichten der Mythologie und ihre Erforschung." *Universitas* (Stuttgart), IX (1954).

――――. "Symbolismus in der antiken Religion." In: *Filosofia e Simbolismo.* (Archivio di Filosofia, Istituto di studi filosofici, Università di Roma.) Rome, 1956; also in *Griechische Miniaturen,* q.v.

――――. "Telesphoros: Zum Verständnis etruskischer, griechischer, und keltisch-germanischer Dämongestalten." *Egyetemes Philologiai Közlöny* (Budapest), LVII (1933).

――――. *Tochter der Sonne.* Zurich, 1944.

――――. *Umgang mit Göttlichem.* Göttingen, 1955.

Kerényi, C. "Wolf und Ziege am Fest der Lupercalia." In: *Mélanges de philologie, de littérature et d'histoire ancienne offerts à Jules Marouzeau.* Paris, 1948.

————. See also Jung, C. G.

Kirsten, E. "Trikka." *RE,* ser. 2, VII.

Koch, Carl. *Gestirnverehrung im alten Italien.* (FrStudRKA, 3.) Frankfurt am Main, 1933.

————. *Der römische Juppiter.* (FrStudRKA, 14.) Frankfurt am Main, 1937.

Kretschmer, Paul. "Semele und Dionysos." In: *Aus der Anomia: Archäologische Beiträge, Carl Robert zur Erinnerung an Berlin dargebracht.* Berlin, 1890.

————. Review of Γ. Χατζιδάκις (G. Khatzidakis), Περὶ τοῦ ἑλληνισμοῦ τῶν ἀρχαίων Μακεδόνων (Athens, 1925). *Glotta* (Göttingen), XVI (1927).

Kubitschek, Wilhelm. *Grundriss der antiken Zeitrechnung.* (Handbuch der Altertumswissenschaft, sec. I, pt. 7.) Munich, 1928.

Kutsch, Ferdinand. *Attische Heilgötter und Heilheroen.* (Religionsgeschichtliche Versuche und Vorarbeiten, XII, pt. 3.) Giessen, 1913.

Lajard, Felix. "Recherches sur le culte du cyprès pyramidal chez les peuples civilisés de l'antiquité." *Mémoires de l'Académie des inscriptions et belles-lettres* [Institut de France], XX, pt. 2 (1854).

Lawrence, D. H. *Apocalypse.* London, 1932.

Lenormant, C., and de Witte, J. *Elite des monuments céramographiques: Matériaux pour l'histoire des religions et des mœurs dans l'antiquité.* Paris, 1844–61. 8 vols. (Especially II, 353–59, pl. civ.)

Leutsch, E. L., and Schneidewin, F. G. (eds.). *Corpus paroemiographorum graecorum.* Gottingen, 1839–51. 2 vols. (Especially II.)

"Little Iliad, The." In: *Hesiod, the Homeric Hymns, and Homerica,* q.v. (under Hesiod).

Livy (Titus Livius). *History of Rome.* With an English translation by B. O. Foster. (LCL.) 1919 ff. 14 vols. (Especially Bk. ii, in I; Bk. iv, in II; Bk. x and Periocha xi, in IV; Bk. xl, in XII.)

LUCIAN. *Skythes*. For an English translation by H. W. Fowler and F. G. Fowler, see "The Scythian." In: *The Works of Lucian of Samosata*. Oxford, 1905. 4 vols. (In II, 102–9.)

MAAS, PAUL. *Epidaurische Hymnen*. (Schriften der Königsberger Gelehrten Gesellschaft für Geisteswissenschaft, Klasse 9, 5.) Halle, 1953.

MACROBIUS. [*Saturnalia*.] Edited by Franz Eyssenhardt. Leipzig, 1893.

MARELLA, M. "Notizie intorno a 5 statue rinvenute nell'Isola Tiberina." *Notizie degli scavi di antichità* (Rome), 1943.

MEIER, CARL ALFRED. *Antike Inkubation und moderne Psychotherapie*. (Studien aus dem C. G. Jung Institut, 1.) Zurich, 1949.

MODONA, A. NEPPI. *L'Isola di Coo nell'antichità classica*. (Memorie dell'Istituto storico-archeologico di Rodi, 1.) Rhodes, 1933.

MÜRI, WALTER. *Der Arzt im Altertum*. Munich, 1938.

MURR, JOSEF. *Die Pflanzenwelt in der griechischen Mythologie*. Innsbruck, 1890.

NEUGEBAUER, KARL ANTON. *Asklepios: Ein Beitrag zur Kritik römischer Statuenkopieen*. (Winckelmannsprogramm der Archäologischen Gesellschaft zu Berlin, 78.) Berlin, 1921.

NILSSON, MARTIN P. *Geschichte der griechischen Religion*. (Handbuch der Altertumswissenschaft, ed. Walter Otto, sec. 5, pt. 2, I–II.) Munich, 1941–50. 2 vols. (Especially I.)

———. *Griechische Feste von religiöser Bedeutung mit Ausschluss der Attischen*. Leipzig, 1906.

NOACK, FERDINAND. "Der Kernbau der Tholos von Epidauros." *JDAI*, XLII (1927).

OTTO, WALTER F. "Apollon." *Neues Abendland* (Augsburg), IV (1949).

———. *Dionysos: Mythos und Kultus*. (FrStudRKA, 4.) 2nd edn., Frankfurt am Main, 1933.

———. *The Homeric Gods*. Translated by Moses Hadas. New York and London, 1955.

———. *Die Manen, oder Von den Urformen des Totenglaubens*. Berlin, 1923.

OTTO, WALTER F. *Die Musen und der göttliche Ursprung des Singens und Sagens.* Düsseldorf, 1955.

———. "Religio und Superstitio." *ArchRW*, XIV (1911).

———. *Theophania: Der Geist der altgriechischen Religion.* (Rowohlts deutsche Enzyklopädie, 15.) Hamburg, 1956.

OVID (PUBLIUS OVIDIUS NASO). *Metamorphoses.* Translated by Rolfe Humphries. Bloomington, Indiana, 1957.

PALMER, L. R. "Observations on the Linear 'B' Tablets from Mycenae." *BullICSLon,* II (1955).

PATON, WILLIAM R., and HICKS, EDWARD LEE. *The Inscriptions of Cos.* Oxford, 1891.

PAUSANIAS. *Description of Greece.* Translated, with a commentary, by J. G. Frazer. London, 1898. 2nd edn., London, 1913. 6 vols. (Especially I, the translation, and III, commentary on Bks. II–V.)

PAZZINI, ADALBERTO. "Il Significato degli 'ex voto' ed il concetto della divinità guaritrice." *RendLinc,* ser. 6a, XI (1935).

PEUCKERT. "Krähe." In *Handwörterbuch des deutschen Aberglaubens,* q.v. (In V.)

———. "Rabe." Ibid. (In VII.)

PHILIPPSON, PAULA. *Thessalische Mythologie.* Zurich, 1944.

PINDAR. *The Odes, including the Principal Fragments.* With an English translation by Sir John Sandys. (LCL.) 1957.

———. *Pindari Carmina cum fragmentis.* Edited by C. M. Bowra. 2nd edn., Oxford, 1947.

PLATO. *Phaedo.* In: *Euthyphro,* etc. ([Collected Works], I.) With an English translation by H. N. Fowler. (LCL.) 1953.

PLINY (GAIUS PLINIUS SECUNDUS). *Natural History.* With an English translation by H. Rackham and W. H. S. Jones. (LCL.) 1938 ff. 10 vols. (Especially Bk. XVI, in IV.)

PLUTARCH. *De defectu oraculorum*, "The Obsolescence of Oracles." In: *Moralia*. Edited, with an English translation, by Frank Cole Babbitt and H. N. Fowler. (LCL.) 1927 ff. 15 vols. (In V.)

————. *De EI*, "The E at Delphi." Ibid. (In V.)

————. "Publicola." In: *Parallel Lives*. With an English translation by Bernadotte Perrin. (LCL.) 1914–26. 11 vols. (In I.)

————. *Quaestiones graecae*. In: *Moralia*. For other details, see above under *De defectu oraculorum*. (In IV.)

————. *Quaestiones romanae*. Ibid. (In IV.)

PRELLER, LUDWIG, and ROBERT, CARL. *Griechische Mythologie*. Berlin, 1887–1926. 2 vols. in 6 parts.

PROPERTIUS, SEXTUS. *Elegies*. With an English translation by H. E. Butler. (LCL.) 1924.

ROBERT, FERNAND. *Thymélè: Recherches sur la signification et la destination des monuments circulaires dans l'architecture religieuse de la Grèce*. (Bibliothèque des Ecoles françaises d'Athènes et de Rome, fasc. 147.) Paris, 1940.

ROHDE, ERWIN. *Psyche*. Translated by W. B. Hillis. London, 1925.

ROSCHER, W. H. "Enneadische Studien." *Abhandlungen der sächsischen Gesellschaft der Wissenschaften*, Philologisch-historische Klasse (Leipzig), XXVI (1907).

SCHAZMANN, PAUL. *Asklepieion*. (Archäologisches Institut des deutschen Reichs. *Kos, I*. Edited by Rudolf Herzog.) Berlin, 1932.

SCHEFOLD, KARL. *Die Bildnisse der antiken Dichter, Redner und Denker*. Basel, 1943.

SCHMIDT, ERNST. *Kultübertragungen*. (Religionsgeschichtliche Versuche und Vorarbeiten, VIII, pt. 2.) Giessen, 1909.

SCHMIDT, JOHANNES. "Telesphoros I." In: W. H. ROSCHER (ed.). *Ausfürliches Lexikon der griechischen und römischen Mythologie*. Leipzig, 1884–1937. 6 vols. in 9 parts, with 2 suppls. (In V.)

SCHMIDT, WILHELM. *Der Ursprung der Gottesidee*. Münster, 1926–55. 12 vols.

SCHUMACHER, JOSEPH. *Antike Medizin*. Berlin, 1940. (Only I published.)

[SERVIUS.] *Commentarii in Virgilium.* . . . Edited by H. Albertus Lion. Göttingen, 1826. 2 vols. (Especially Bks. III and X, in I.)

Spirit and Nature (Papers from the Eranos Yearbooks, 1; ed. Joseph Campbell). (Bollingen Series XXX.) New York, 1954; London, 1955.

STÄHLIN, FRIEDRICH. *Das hellenische Thessalien.* Stuttgart, 1924.

STRABO. *The Geography.* With an English translation by Horace Leonard Jones. (LCL.) 1917–32. 8 vols. (Especially Bk. XIV, in VI.)

SUETONIUS (GAIUS SUETONIUS TRANQUILLUS). "The Deified Claudius." In: *The Lives of the Caesars.* With an English translation by J. C. Rolfe. (LCL.) 1914. 2 vols. (Especially Bk. V, in II.)

TISCHBEIN, WILLIAM (ed.). *Collection of Engravings from Ancient Vases of Greek Workmanship . . . in the Possession of Sir Wm. Hamilton.* Naples, 1791–95. 3 vols. (Especially II, pl. 17.)

USENER, HERMANN. *Götternamen.* Bonn, 1896.

———. "Mythologie." *ArchRW,* VII (1904).

VALERIUS MAXIMUS. *Factorum et dictorum memorabilium libri novem.* Edited by Karl Kempf, Leipzig, 1888.

VENTRIS, MICHAEL, and CHADWICK, JOHN. "Evidence for Greek Dialect in the Mycenaean Archives." *JHS,* LXXIII (1953).

VITRUVIUS POLLIO. *The Ten Books on Architecture.* Edited, with an English translation, by Frank Granger. (LCL.) 1931–34. 2 vols. (Especially Bk. I, in I.)

WALDAPFEL, IMRE. "Martyr occultus." *Lyka-Emlékkönyv* (Budapest), 1944. (In Hungarian.)

WEBER, LEO. "Asklepios, älteste Zeugnisse aus Thessalien und der Peloponnes." *Philologus,* LXXXVII [N.S. XLI] (1932).

WEINREICH, OTTO. *Antike Heilungswunder: Untersuchungen zum Wunderglauben der Griechen und Römer.* (Religionsgeschichtliche Versuche und Vorarbeiten, VIII, pt. 1.) Giessen, 1909.

———. "Relationes de sanationibus," nos. 1168–73. In: *Sylloge inscriptionum graecarum,* edited by Wilhelm Dittenberger. 3rd edn., Leipzig, 1915–20. 4 vols. (In III, 310–33.)

WELLMANN, M. "Augenärzte." *RE*, II.

———. "Drakon." *RE*, V.

WILAMOWITZ-MOELLENDORFF, ULRICH VON. *Der Glaube der Hellenen.* Berlin, 1931–32. 2 vols. (Especially II.)

———. *Isyllos von Epidauros.* (Philologische Untersuchungen, 9.) Berlin, 1886.

———. "Neue lesbische Lyrik." *Neue Jahrbücher für das klassische Altertum* (Leipzig), XXXIII (1914).

WISSOWA, GEORG. *Religion und Kultus der Römer.* (Handbuch der klassischen Altertumswissenschaft, V, pt. 4.) 2nd edn., Munich, 1912.

WOLTERS, PAUL. "Darstellungen des Asklepios." *AM*, XVII (1892).

WÜNSCH, RICHARD. "Ein Dankopfer an Asklepios." *ArchRW*, VII (1904).

ZIEHEN, JULIUS. "Über die Lage des Asklepiosheiligtums von Trikka." *AM*, XVII (1892).

INDEX

An asterisk indicates an illustration on the page cited; a superior figure (e.g., 114 [4]), a note likewise on the page cited.